Baba Vanga Prophecies for 2025

Andrew Parry

Published by Andrew Parry, 2024.

BABA VANGA PROPHECIES FOR 2025

First edition. November 15, 2024.

ISBN: 979-8230662426

Written by Andrew Parry.

Table of Contents

Introduction to Prophecy: A Timeless Fascination 1

The Legacy of Baba Vanga: A Prophet for the Ages 3

Baba Vanga's Early Life and Path to Clairvoyance 5

The Mystique behind Baba Vanga's Predictions 7

Exploring the Process: How Baba Vanga Foretold the Future 9

The Importance of the Year 2025 in Baba Vanga's Predictions 11

Baba Vanga's Prophecies: Reliability and Skepticism 13

Global Perspectives on Prophecy and Predictions... 15

What Do Prophecies Mean for Modern Society? 18

The Relevance of Prophecy in Today's World Affairs 21

A First Look at 2025: Key Predictions and Their Themes 24

Natural Disasters Foretold for 2025 26

Environmental Challenges and Climate Crisis in 2025 28

The Shifting Poles: Is a Geomagnetic Flip Coming?.. 31

Baba Vanga's Vision of Earthquakes and Volcanic Eruptions................................. 34

Water Crises and Floods: Baba Vanga's Warnings for 2025 37

Famine and Scarcity: A Global Food Crisis on the Horizon? 40

Economic Predictions for 2025: Recession or Recovery?.. 43

Political Upheavals: Are Major Governments Destined to Collapse? 46

Baba Vanga's Views on Technological Advancements in 2025 49

Artificial Intelligence: Friend or Foe According to Baba Vanga? 52

Human Cloning and Genetic Manipulation: A 2025 Reality? 55

Baba Vanga's Take on Space Exploration and Discoveries....................................... 58

Alien Contact: Did Baba Vanga Predict Interplanetary Encounters?...................... 61

Social Unrest and Civil Disobedience in 2025.. 64

Youth Movements and the Rise of a New World Order... 67

The Spiritual Awakening of Humanity in 2025 70

The Role of Religion and Spirituality in the New World 73

Baba Vanga on Health Pandemics and Medical Advancements 76

Disease Outbreaks and the Potential for a Global Pandemic 79

Global Power Shifts: East Meets West in Baba Vanga's Prophecies 82

The Digital Economy and Cryptocurrency Predictions 85

The Impact of Climate Refugees: A Humanitarian Crisis? 89

Nuclear Tensions and the Threat of a New Arms Race 92

Baba Vanga on the Rise of New Superpowers 95

Technological Utopia or Dystopia: Baba Vanga's Insights 99

Energy Wars: The Battle for Resources in 2025 103

Bioengineering and the Ethical Implications of 2025 107

The Future of Education According to Baba Vanga 111

Global Unification or Fragmentation? Baba Vanga's Vision 115

Prophecies on the Changing Role of Women in Society 119

The Balance of Nature: Ecological Harmony or Destruction? 123

Baba Vanga on the Role of Media and Truth in 2025 127

The Emergence of New Philosophies and Belief Systems 131

Global Consciousness: The Unification of Minds and Souls 134

Baba Vanga's Warning to Humanity: What Lies Ahead? 137

Interpreting Baba Vanga's Predictions in Light of 2024 Events 140

Science and Prophecy: How Modern Data Aligns with Predictions 143

Reflections on Baba Vanga's 2025 and Beyond 146

Baba Vanga's Prophecies about Donald Trump in 2025 149

Conclusion: What Does Baba Vanga's Legacy Mean for Our Future? 151

Introduction to Prophecy: A Timeless Fascination

From the earliest whispers of human civilization, prophecy has held a unique place in our collective imagination. The notion that certain individuals possess the ability to glimpse beyond the veil of the present into the mysteries of the future has captivated minds across cultures and generations. Prophecy, often linked to spiritual insight, is found in nearly every major civilization—from the Oracle of Delphi in Ancient Greece to the cryptic prophecies of Nostradamus in Renaissance Europe and, more recently, the predictions of Baba Vanga in Eastern Europe. Each of these figures has inspired awe, skepticism, and even fear, raising questions about destiny, fate, and free will.

The appeal of prophecy lies in its dual role: it provides both a sense of mystery and a semblance of control. The desire to know what the future holds is deeply rooted in the human psyche, as it offers reassurance and, paradoxically, a way to prepare for the unknown. Prophecies are more than just forecasts; they are reflections of our greatest hopes and fears, woven into predictions that transcend time. In seeking prophecies, people often hope to find insights that might guide their actions, validate their beliefs, or simply bring comfort in times of uncertainty.

In ancient societies, prophets and seers held prominent roles, often guiding political and spiritual decisions. The Greeks consulted oracles before battles, and in Rome, augurs interpreted the will of the gods by observing natural signs. These prophets were revered as intermediaries between the human and the divine, believed to possess gifts granted by deities or forces beyond human comprehension. For these societies, prophecies were not mere predictions but glimpses into an ordered universe, where every event, no matter how chaotic, followed a divine plan.

Despite advancements in science and technology, prophecy remains relevant today, evolving into new forms while preserving its essential allure. In contemporary society, prophets might appear as mystics, futurists, or even scientists—those who predict trends and developments based on patterns they discern. Although many people turn to science for explanations, a significant number still seek answers in the mystical and unexplained, finding comfort in the belief that there are forces at work beyond our understanding.

The rise of modern media has only intensified our fascination with prophecy. Predictions about climate change, economic trends, and political shifts dominate headlines, showing that the desire for foreknowledge has merely transformed rather than diminished. These "modern prophecies" play on the same desires that ancient seers tapped into, providing both a warning and a vision of hope for those who seek them.

Among modern prophets, Baba Vanga stands out as a unique figure. A blind Bulgarian mystic, her life story is as compelling as her predictions. Over decades, she gained a reputation for foreseeing events with startling accuracy, from geopolitical shifts to natural disasters. Baba Vanga's reputation has grown posthumously, and she is often compared to famous historical prophets due to the breadth and impact of her predictions. Known as "the Nostradamus of the Balkans," she occupies a place in the hearts of believers who see her as a beacon of wisdom and foresight.

The allure of Baba Vanga's predictions lies not only in their accuracy but also in her humble origins and the simplicity of her life. Her prophecies cover a vast range of topics—from global disasters and technological advancements to spiritual awakenings and encounters with extraterrestrial life. In a world increasingly driven by scientific evidence, her life and legacy remind us that there remains a deep, unyielding fascination with the mystical and unknown.

This book explores the predictions of Baba Vanga for the year 2025, examining them through the lens of current world events and scientific understanding. By analyzing her forecasts in the context of our modern world, we aim to uncover the threads of relevance they may hold for contemporary society. Does prophecy still serve a purpose in an age dominated by reason? Or, perhaps more intriguingly, do Baba Vanga's predictions offer insights into possibilities that even modern science has yet to uncover?

As we delve into each prediction, we must remember that prophecy is not always precise; it is open to interpretation and often shrouded in ambiguity. Baba Vanga's visions, much like those of other famous prophets, are at times vague and symbolic. They challenge us to look beyond the literal and to ponder the deeper meanings hidden within. In doing so, we are invited into a journey of reflection, where we confront both the known and the unknown, seeking to reconcile the mysteries of fate with the logic of our modern age.

The chapters that follow will take you through a year brimming with potential transformation, guided by the visions of Baba Vanga. Whether you are a skeptic, a believer, or simply curious, the predictions for 2025 promise to be a compelling exploration into the boundaries of human understanding, a journey that may inspire new perspectives on what it means to glimpse the future.

The Legacy of Baba Vanga: A Prophet for the Ages

Baba Vanga's story is as enigmatic as the predictions she left behind. Born Vangeliya Pandeva Dimitrova in 1911 in a small village in Bulgaria, her journey from a humble peasant life to an internationally renowned seer is filled with events that border on the mythical. Known for her sharp wit and humble wisdom, Baba Vanga, often referred to simply as "Baba," which means "grandmother" in Bulgarian, remains one of the most beloved and controversial figures in the world of prophecy. To her followers, she was not only a prophet but also a compassionate figure who offered solace and guidance in a world often marred by turmoil.

The story of Baba Vanga's rise as a mystic begins with a pivotal moment in her early life—a violent storm that swept her off her feet and blinded her with sand and debris. Although tragic, this event was perceived by many as an initiation into her mystical abilities. According to accounts, after this accident, she began experiencing visions, hearing voices, and perceiving the world in ways that others could not. Her blindness, rather than hindering her, became a symbol of her otherworldly sight, granting her a connection to the unseen.

As her abilities became known, people from all over the Balkans and beyond flocked to her, seeking answers to questions about their lives, families, and futures. Her small home in Petrich, Bulgaria, became a place of pilgrimage, with hundreds lining up each day in hopes of a moment with her. Whether they were peasants or politicians, they came with deep questions, and many left with profound insights—answers that, for better or worse, had a lasting impact on their lives.

One of the most intriguing aspects of Baba Vanga's predictions is the sheer scope of her visions. Unlike many prophets who focused on specific events or limited themselves to personal matters, Baba Vanga's prophecies spanned global themes, touching on politics, natural disasters, scientific advancements, and spiritual awakenings. Her predictions often addressed the fate of nations and the trajectory of humanity, bringing her recognition as an extraordinary figure. She is known to have predicted the breakup of the Soviet Union, the Chernobyl disaster, and even the events of September 11, 2001. Her accuracy in foreseeing some major global events has left many in awe and earned her the moniker "the Nostradamus of the Balkans."

Despite her reputation, Baba Vanga was a humble person who did not seek fame. She often cautioned people about interpreting her words too literally, emphasizing that her visions came to her in ways that were sometimes symbolic, layered in metaphor, or obscure. She spoke with a simplicity that was both cryptic and profound, often using images and analogies that could be interpreted in multiple ways. This ambiguity, while it attracted followers, also fueled skepticism. Critics argue that her predictions are too vague, relying on open-ended language that could apply to many scenarios. Yet her dedicated followers insist that her insights have proven accurate time and again, especially when examined in the light of current events.

Baba Vanga's influence extends far beyond the realms of prophecy and mysticism. In the Balkan region, she is revered as a cultural icon, a source of national pride, and a spiritual leader. People continue to visit her home, now a museum, where they leave offerings and seek guidance in her memory. Her name has become synonymous with Bulgaria's mystical heritage, and she is often seen as a bridge between the traditional and modern worlds, a figure who embodies the wisdom of ancient practices in a rapidly changing age.

What makes Baba Vanga's legacy truly remarkable is the way she brought people from different backgrounds together. She saw no barriers between rich and poor, educated and uneducated, believers and skeptics. Her humble home became a gathering place for those searching for meaning, and her words resonated with a deep humanity that transcended social divides. To her followers, Baba Vanga was not only a prophet but also a compassionate soul who genuinely cared for the well-being of others. This empathy and concern for humanity is a key part of her legacy, one that has contributed to her enduring influence.

Today, Baba Vanga's legacy continues through her predictions and the mystery surrounding them. Her prophecies, particularly those pertaining to future years like 2025, have gained renewed attention. As the world grapples with uncertainty—from environmental crises to political instability and the rapid rise of technology—her visions serve as a touchstone for reflection. For believers, her predictions offer a sense of forewarning and even a path forward, as they seek to align their lives with the wisdom she imparted. For skeptics, she remains an enigmatic figure, an example of the power of belief and the human tendency to seek patterns and meaning, even in the face of the inexplicable.

Baba Vanga's story is also a testament to the resilience of tradition in a modern world. In an era dominated by science and skepticism, her enduring popularity speaks to a deep, primal need for connection with the unknown, a reminder that not all questions can be answered by rationality alone. Her life and work have sparked numerous debates, inspired documentaries, and continue to be subjects of study. Scholars and laypeople alike are drawn to her story, exploring how she navigated the balance between the mystical and the mundane.

As we explore her predictions for 2025, we carry with us the understanding that Baba Vanga's legacy is more than a series of prophecies; it is a reminder of the interconnectedness of all things. Her life encourages us to reflect on the mysteries of fate and destiny and to ponder the limitations of human perception. Whether her visions for the future are literal truths or allegorical messages, they offer a lens through which we can examine our present world, prompting us to question, reflect, and perhaps find our own meaning in the unfolding story of humanity.

Baba Vanga's Early Life and Path to Clairvoyance

Baba Vanga's journey from an ordinary child to one of the world's most enigmatic prophets is filled with elements that seem almost destined. Born Vangeliya Pandeva Dimitrova on January 31, 1911, in Strumica—then part of the Ottoman Empire and now located in modern-day North Macedonia—her childhood was one marked by poverty, hardship, and an unshakable resilience that would come to define her life. Her early years provide a glimpse into the struggles and cultural roots that shaped her, laying the foundation for her eventual role as a spiritual guide and seer.

Vanga's family faced significant hardships, starting with the untimely loss of her mother shortly after her birth. This left her in the care of her father, who, due to political unrest and constant changes in the ruling powers of the region, struggled to make ends meet. Vanga's father, a soldier during World War I, was imprisoned for his pro-Bulgarian political stance, leaving her in the care of neighbors. Raised in a humble setting with little material comfort, Vanga's childhood was one marked by survival and the need to develop strength of character.

Her first known brush with the mystical came when she was just a child. Vanga was reportedly fascinated by "healing herbs" and showed an early interest in assisting those around her who were suffering from minor ailments. It's said that she displayed an intuitive ability to select specific herbs and plants to help the sick, a skill often associated with folk medicine traditions in the region. This budding instinct for healing was an early hint of the unique path that lay ahead of her.

The transformative event in Vanga's life, however, occurred when she was just twelve years old. In a story that has become the cornerstone of her mystical narrative, Vanga was caught in a powerful storm while walking through her village. The fierce winds whipped up dirt and sand, which blinded her as she was thrown to the ground by the storm's force. When the winds subsided, her family found her, terrified and disoriented, unable to open her eyes. The damage to her eyes was severe, and, due to her family's poverty, she was unable to access the medical care that might have saved her vision.

This incident left Vanga permanently blind, a loss that was both profound and symbolic. Though tragic, her blindness became a defining feature of her life and spiritual identity. In many spiritual traditions, blindness is viewed as a metaphorical gateway to inner sight—a condition that frees the mind to see beyond the physical world. Vanga's blindness seemed to open her to another realm, one where she could perceive things invisible to others. She later described her visions as "pictures in her mind," accompanied by voices and sensations that allowed her to "see" events, both near and far, past and future.

Her path to clairvoyance did not happen overnight. The years following her accident were challenging, as she adjusted to life without sight. She attended a school for the blind in the Serbian town of Zemun, where she learned essential life skills such as Braille, playing the piano, and cooking, as well as nurturing her independence. Though she was able to function capably in daily life, Vanga's mystical abilities began to grow stronger, gaining prominence within her small community.

By her late teens, Vanga had started to offer insights to those who sought her out. At first, these predictions were humble—offering guidance on lost items or insights into personal struggles. Her reputation began to spread, as people marveled at her accuracy and the way she seemed to "know" details that were impossible for an ordinary person to discern. What initially started as small acts of service grew into a larger calling, as her visions became clearer and more encompassing.

As her abilities gained recognition, so too did the scope of her visions. By the time she reached adulthood, her insights had evolved from local matters to events that spanned regions and eventually, the world. During World War II, her fame as a prophet grew, as people sought her counsel about loved ones who were missing in action or the fate of their towns and villages. Her predictions during this time were eerily precise, and she reportedly foresaw certain battles and the outcomes of military campaigns. This accuracy further cemented her reputation, and her humble home began to draw visitors from far and wide.

It was around this time that her life took another turn, as Vanga herself experienced a vision of the Virgin Mary, whom she claimed gave her a mission to guide and counsel humanity. Following this vision, Vanga's commitment to her spiritual role deepened, and she became known not only as a prophet but also as a healer and advisor. She welcomed everyone, from villagers to high-ranking officials, who sought her wisdom. She never charged for her services, seeing her gift as something to be freely shared with those in need.

Vanga's journey to clairvoyance was as much about her personal trials as it was about her abilities. Her blindness, far from limiting her, became the key that opened the door to her unique form of sight. Her modest upbringing instilled in her a strong sense of empathy and compassion, qualities that drew people to her and allowed them to trust her with their deepest concerns. Her early struggles and her extraordinary perseverance shaped her into a figure of strength and wisdom, deeply rooted in the cultural and spiritual traditions of her homeland.

By the end of her life, Baba Vanga had evolved from a simple village girl into a cultural icon, known across Eastern Europe and beyond. Her followers remember her not only for her prophecies but for the warmth and humility with which she served others. Her early life, filled with adversity, created the foundation for her mystical path, a journey that would lead her to become a beacon of insight for countless individuals around the world. In examining her path to clairvoyance, we begin to understand the forces that shaped Baba Vanga's extraordinary life and the enduring legacy she left behind.

The Mystique behind Baba Vanga's Predictions

Baba Vanga's predictions have fascinated, mystified, and even unsettled people worldwide. What makes her prophecies so captivating is the aura of mystique that surrounds them—an air of both ambiguity and astonishing precision. Unlike scientific forecasts based on data and trends, Baba Vanga's predictions came to her as visions, often laced with metaphor and open to interpretation. Understanding the mystique behind her prophecies requires a deep dive into her unique process, her spiritual beliefs, and the power of symbolism woven into her visions.

The process by which Baba Vanga received her visions is a source of intrigue. She did not employ conventional methods of forecasting or rely on tools like tarot cards, astrology, or numerology. Instead, her prophecies arrived spontaneously, often described as vivid mental images accompanied by strong sensations or an inner voice. She would see "pictures" or "scenes" in her mind, sometimes as if watching events unfold like a movie, and would feel compelled to share what she had "seen." These visions could be triggered by a simple question or arrive unbidden, flashing before her mind with an immediacy that left no room for doubt.

The exact source of Baba Vanga's visions remains a mystery. Some attribute her abilities to divine intervention, suggesting that she was a medium through which higher powers communicated with humanity. Baba Vanga herself claimed to receive guidance from spiritual forces, often mentioning the presence of unseen beings who "spoke" to her. These entities, she said, offered her glimpses into the future, allowing her to warn or advise people based on what they revealed to her. Her followers believe that she was chosen for this gift, her blindness seen as a form of spiritual compensation, allowing her to see beyond the physical world into realms hidden from ordinary sight.

One of the most remarkable aspects of Baba Vanga's prophecies is their breadth. Unlike many prophets who focus on local or personal matters, Baba Vanga's visions touched on global events, major political shifts, natural disasters, technological advancements, and even intergalactic phenomena. This scope has led some to believe that her consciousness was attuned to a higher, universal frequency, one that transcended human limitations. Her predictions for the 21st century, in particular, seem to anticipate challenges humanity faces today, from climate change to geopolitical tensions and the ethical quandaries surrounding technology and artificial intelligence.

The mystique of Baba Vanga's predictions also lies in their ambiguity. Often, she spoke in cryptic language, using symbols and metaphors that left her prophecies open to various interpretations. For instance, when she described a "great wave" or a "wall of water," it was only years later, after the 2004 Indian Ocean tsunami, that people connected her words to the disaster. Similarly, her vision of "steel birds attacking the twin brothers" was widely interpreted as a forewarning of the September 11, 2001 attacks on the World Trade Center. Yet these interpretations come in hindsight, and her prophecies remain flexible enough to be reinterpreted as events unfold, adding a layer of mystique and speculation.

This flexibility in interpretation has fueled skepticism as well as belief. Critics argue that her prophecies are often so vague that they could fit many different events, thus diminishing their reliability. Yet her followers maintain that the symbolism in her visions was necessary, as it allowed her to communicate ideas that were otherwise difficult to articulate. In this sense, her prophecies resemble parables—stories or images that carry deeper truths, waiting to be unlocked by those who seek them earnestly.

Baba Vanga's prophecies are also deeply rooted in the cultural and spiritual traditions of the Balkans, a region rich in folklore and mysticism. The idea of a seer or a wise woman—a "baba" in Slavic culture—is not uncommon, and Baba

Vanga is often seen as a continuation of this tradition. Her use of natural elements in her prophecies, from rivers and mountains to storms and animals, resonates with the earth-centered spirituality that characterizes much of Balkan folk culture. For many of her followers, her predictions are more than just forecasts; they are reflections of ancient wisdom, tapping into a primal knowledge of the cycles and forces of nature.

Her fame grew, in part, because her predictions resonated on an emotional level. She often spoke with an urgency that conveyed her concern for humanity, warning against human hubris and the disregard for nature. She predicted dire consequences for those who pursued paths of greed, violence, and exploitation, urging people to live in harmony with the earth and one another. This moral dimension adds depth to her legacy, transforming her from a mere prognosticator into a spiritual guide, one whose visions serve as moral cautionary tales for modern society.

There is also a profound mystery in how her prophecies seemed to foreshadow technological advancements and global shifts long before they became feasible. Her visions of artificial intelligence, interstellar contact, and genetic engineering seem astonishingly prescient given the technological landscape of her time. Many wonder how a blind woman, living in a small Balkan village with minimal exposure to the outside world, could speak of future scientific advancements with such conviction. This element of her story lends a near-mythical quality to her prophecies, suggesting that her consciousness was somehow attuned to a realm beyond time and space.

Some scientists and researchers have attempted to study her predictions, seeking a rational explanation for her accuracy. While no concrete evidence has been found to explain the phenomenon of her visions, Baba Vanga remains a subject of interest, even to those rooted in science and skepticism. Her life and work have been examined through psychological and parapsychological lenses, with some theorizing that her heightened intuition was a product of her sensory deprivation, while others suggest she may have tapped into a form of collective consciousness. Yet, even with these explanations, the core mystery remains. For believers, Baba Vanga's visions are a testament to the limits of human understanding, a reminder that there are forces beyond our comprehension that shape our lives and the world around us. Her prophecies are seen as glimpses into a hidden order of existence, one that defies the boundaries of rational thought and invites us to ponder the mysteries of destiny and free will. Her prophecies invite us into a realm where past, present, and future converge, where symbols and signs hint at truths that elude direct understanding. By embracing the mystery, we are reminded of the limitations of human knowledge and the vast unknown that lies just beyond our reach.

Exploring the Process: How Baba Vanga Foretold the Future

The method by which Baba Vanga received her prophecies is one of the most captivating aspects of her legacy. Unlike conventional prophets or mystics who use tools like tarot cards, astrology charts, or crystal balls, Baba Vanga's process of "seeing" the future was organic, intuitive, and often spontaneous. Her ability to foretell future events was marked by a series of unusual sensory experiences that seemed to provide her with a window into realities beyond normal perception. In this chapter, we delve into the unique process that shaped her clairvoyance, exploring both her accounts of the phenomenon and interpretations that have emerged from her followers, researchers, and skeptics alike.

Baba Vanga described her visions as "pictures in her mind," flashes of scenes or images that would appear without warning. Often, she would receive these visions in moments of stillness or when someone asked her a specific question. Unlike dreamlike images, which are often vague and chaotic, Baba Vanga's visions appeared to her as vivid, fully-formed sequences. Sometimes, she felt a strong physical sensation accompanying these images, which she likened to an overwhelming wave of emotion or a sense of intense energy passing through her. These experiences varied in intensity; some left her feeling exhausted, while others seemed to fill her with a serene sense of certainty.

There was a distinctly mystical quality to her visions. Baba Vanga claimed that she often heard voices, not in the way one would hear a person speaking, but as an inner dialogue or an impression left in her mind. She believed these voices were guiding spirits or entities that granted her insight into events that were unfolding or yet to come. For her, these voices were more than just thoughts or impulses; they were messages from a higher plane of consciousness, communicating truths that defied human logic and temporal constraints. This spiritual connection was a vital part of her process, as she often referred to these entities as her "guides" who helped her fulfill her mission.

One fascinating aspect of Baba Vanga's process was her symbolic interpretation of events. Her visions were often loaded with metaphor and imagery, which she believed were essential to understanding the true nature of her prophecies. For instance, she might see an eagle soaring over a stormy sea, which could symbolize a powerful nation navigating a period of turmoil. This symbolic nature of her visions required interpretation, adding a layer of complexity that often made her predictions both mysterious and open to multiple readings. She was known to say that her visions were "like pieces of a puzzle" that had to be carefully pieced together to reveal their full meaning.

Baba Vanga's own explanations of her visions were humble and grounded. She did not claim to understand why she was chosen or how the process worked; she simply accepted it as a part of her life. She often expressed gratitude for her ability but also admitted that it was a heavy burden to carry. Seeing glimpses of potential disasters or tragedies weighed on her, especially when the details were unclear, leaving her unable to prevent what she foresaw. This ethical dilemma, the tension between knowing and being powerless to act, was a recurring theme in her life, and she saw her role as a warning voice rather than an agent of change.

To some extent, her blindness played a key role in shaping her process. Deprived of physical sight, Baba Vanga's mind seemed to have heightened other senses, allowing her to focus deeply on the mental and spiritual realms. This sensory deprivation is often linked to heightened intuition and perception, as the mind compensates for a lack of visual input by honing other faculties. Whether by coincidence or divine design, Baba Vanga's blindness became a metaphorical "inner sight," a way of seeing that went beyond the physical. She once remarked that her blindness allowed her to "see what others cannot," suggesting that her loss of ordinary sight was a gateway to her extraordinary visions.

Her followers have long speculated on how her visions might relate to modern concepts like intuition, the subconscious, and even quantum physics. Some theorize that Baba Vanga's mind was able to tap into a "collective consciousness" or a "universal database" that contained information about past, present, and future. According to this theory, her clairvoyance was a result of her attunement to this vast network of information, allowing her to access knowledge that most people are unaware of. In this view, her visions could be seen as a form of psychic intuition heightened to an extraordinary degree, allowing her to connect with truths on a scale beyond individual understanding.

Another interpretation is that Baba Vanga's prophecies were born from an intense empathy, a heightened sensitivity to the energies and emotions of those around her. Her connection to people, her deep compassion, and her ability to perceive hidden fears and desires could have been a key element in her prophetic process. When someone would visit her, she seemed to tune into their essence, picking up on subtle cues, emotions, and even future possibilities. This empathy allowed her to form insights that, though difficult to explain scientifically, resonated deeply with the people she helped, who often reported that she seemed to "know" things she could not possibly have known.

In examining her process, it is also essential to consider the limitations and challenges Baba Vanga faced. Despite her abilities, she was often frustrated by the lack of clarity in some of her visions. She described certain images as blurry or incomplete, as if she were looking through a foggy window. This uncertainty meant that she did not always understand the full implications of what she saw. She often warned people to approach her words with caution, aware that her visions were not infallible and that they required interpretation. This humility and realism added depth to her mystique, as she herself acknowledged the limitations of her gift.

The spontaneity of Baba Vanga's visions, their symbolic nature, and her connection to unseen entities make her process difficult to categorize or replicate. For researchers, her method presents an intriguing case that bridges mysticism, psychology, and spirituality. While some view her process as purely mystical, others attempt to find rational explanations, suggesting that her abilities could have been an extraordinary form of intuition, a heightened sensitivity to patterns and energies that most people overlook.

Ultimately, Baba Vanga's process defies easy explanation, maintaining an aura of mystery that continues to captivate people today. Whether one views her as a mystic touched by the divine or a sensitive individual with a unique gift of perception, her process remains an enigmatic phenomenon that challenges our understanding of reality and time.

Her life and predictions invite us to consider the possibility that knowledge exists beyond the realm of logic, inviting us to explore realms of consciousness that remain largely unexplored.

As we move forward into her predictions for 2025, understanding Baba Vanga's process reminds us that prophecy is not an exact science; it is a mystical journey through realms of intuition and insight that go beyond ordinary experience. Her unique method, while shrouded in mystery, offers a glimpse into the timeless fascination with prophecy—a human endeavor that seeks meaning, guidance, and connection in the vast unknown.

The Importance of the Year 2025 in Baba Vanga's Predictions

The year 2025 holds a unique place within Baba Vanga's prophecies, as she saw it as a pivotal time for humanity—a year of significant change, challenges, and transformation. According to her followers, Baba Vanga described this year as a "turning point," a time when humanity would face choices that could either lead to new heights of unity and understanding or bring further division and hardship. To her, 2025 wasn't merely another year but a moment in history with the potential to reshape our global trajectory.

Baba Vanga's focus on 2025 was not unusual within the world of prophecy. Many prophets and seers have pointed to certain years or time frames as particularly significant, often describing them as periods of "revelation" or "reckoning." This is a recurring theme in mystical traditions, where certain moments in time are believed to hold more transformative energy, aligning with changes in social structures, environmental shifts, or even cosmic cycles. Baba Vanga's visions of 2025 seem to fall into this pattern, marked by her consistent emphasis on this year as a "gateway" to the future of humanity.

One of the main themes Baba Vanga foresaw for 2025 was the rise of technological advancements that would challenge our concepts of ethics, identity, and human connection. She predicted breakthroughs in artificial intelligence, genetic engineering, and even interstellar communication—developments that would push the boundaries of human capability and comprehension. However, she also warned of the dangers these advancements could bring if pursued without moral responsibility. Her visions suggest that in 2025, society would reach a critical juncture: one path leading to a harmonious integration of technology and humanity, the other to a potential loss of control and even conflict.

Another key focus in Baba Vanga's predictions for 2025 was environmental upheaval. Her visions included images of extreme natural disasters—earthquakes, tsunamis, and drastic climate shifts that she believed would force humanity to confront the consequences of decades of environmental neglect. She spoke of "rivers changing their course" and "oceans swelling with power," which many have interpreted as references to climate-induced flooding, shifting weather patterns, and the rise in sea levels. In her view, these natural events were not only a warning but a call for humanity to adopt a more harmonious relationship with the earth, emphasizing that our survival depended on our ability to respect and protect the planet.

Baba Vanga also foresaw 2025 as a time of spiritual awakening, predicting a global "re-evaluation" of values, beliefs, and priorities. She described a movement toward greater unity, compassion, and spiritual awareness, as more people would begin to seek deeper meaning and connection in their lives. This "awakening" would be sparked by the challenges humanity faced, as people would turn inward to find strength, resilience, and purpose amid uncertainty. According to Baba Vanga, this shift in consciousness could be a source of healing for individuals and societies, fostering a renewed commitment to peace and understanding across cultures and nations.

Politically, Baba Vanga envisioned 2025 as a year of significant shifts in global power dynamics. She foresaw new alliances emerging, some that would surprise the world and others that would dissolve after years of instability. Her visions hinted at the rise of new superpowers and the decline of some established ones, suggesting a redistribution of influence that could either stabilize or unsettle the international stage. In her view, this geopolitical shift was closely tied to the ethical challenges posed by technological advancements, with nations needing to cooperate to manage the impact of new technologies responsibly.

Interestingly, Baba Vanga's predictions for 2025 also touched on humanity's relationship with the cosmos. She foresaw an increasing interest in space exploration and the possibility of interplanetary communication. Some interpretations of her visions suggest that she believed humanity would encounter signs of extraterrestrial intelligence or uncover new, significant knowledge about the universe. Whether this was literal or metaphorical remains open to debate, but her focus on the cosmos aligns with the scientific advancements and exploratory spirit humanity has shown in recent years.

While her predictions painted a picture of both challenges and potential breakthroughs, Baba Vanga emphasized that the outcomes of 2025 would depend heavily on human choices. She believed that humanity would be tested—faced with decisions that required wisdom, patience, and humility. Her visions seemed to advocate for a balanced approach, urging humanity to embrace technological progress while remaining rooted in ethical and spiritual values. She warned that neglecting these values could lead to consequences that would ripple far beyond 2025, affecting future generations and the planet as a whole.

The importance of 2025 in Baba Vanga's predictions is perhaps best understood as a call to awareness, a reminder of the interconnectedness of all things. She saw the year as a culmination of past actions and as a decisive moment in humanity's collective story. The potential for drastic changes in environmental, technological, and social spheres underlined her message that we must take responsibility for our choices and actions. Her visions conveyed an urgency, a belief that humanity stood at a crossroads and that 2025 would be the year to choose a path—one that would either lead to harmony and growth or to discord and decline.

In reflecting on these predictions, it's clear that 2025 was not merely a "future" year for Baba Vanga but a focal point through which she viewed the unfolding human story. To her, it represented an opportunity for humanity to redefine itself, to confront the dilemmas brought on by its own innovations and decisions, and to move toward a more enlightened existence. Whether we interpret her prophecies as literal forecasts or allegorical messages, her emphasis on this year invites us to consider the impact of our actions today and the importance of choosing our future wisely.

As we continue to explore Baba Vanga's specific predictions for 2025, we'll see her visions span various domains, each one adding to her portrayal of this year as a crucial turning point. Her predictions prompt us to ask ourselves what kind of future we are creating, urging us to reflect on the choices we make as individuals, communities, and nations.

Baba Vanga's Prophecies: Reliability and Skepticism

Baba Vanga's prophecies have captured the public's imagination, sparking both profound belief and intense skepticism. Her reputation as a seer has grown considerably since her death, with her predictions for global events, natural disasters, and social shifts being dissected and debated by believers and skeptics alike. This chapter delves into the question of reliability surrounding Baba Vanga's prophecies, examining why many consider her predictions credible and why others view her visions with suspicion.

Supporters of Baba Vanga's prophetic abilities argue that her track record speaks for itself. Her predictions about significant events such as the Chernobyl disaster, the 9/11 attacks, and the rise of ISIS have fueled a belief in her extraordinary insight. Followers argue that her accuracy in foretelling these events, often years in advance, points to a genuine ability to glimpse into the future. In these cases, they see not only her skill in prediction but also her compassion for humanity, as she tried to warn of impending disasters. Many of her supporters regard her as a rare individual gifted with a spiritual sight that allowed her to see patterns and trajectories beyond the understanding of ordinary people.

There is also the matter of the consistency of her prophecies, which believers see as evidence of her credibility. Over the years, Baba Vanga reportedly predicted numerous world events, always maintaining a somber and cautious tone. Unlike other alleged prophets who make vague and sporadic predictions, Baba Vanga's visions followed a clear and often detailed theme, touching on topics such as natural disasters, technological advancements, and spiritual awakenings. This consistency has further bolstered her credibility among her followers, who see her not as a fortune teller but as a messenger providing guidance to prepare humanity for the future.

However, despite the confidence of her supporters, Baba Vanga's predictions have not gone unchallenged. Skeptics argue that her prophecies are often ambiguous, open to broad interpretation, and sometimes only seem accurate in hindsight. Many of her predictions are couched in symbolic language, which can be interpreted in various ways depending on context. For instance, her descriptions of "two steel birds" attacking "twin brothers" has widely been interpreted as foreseeing the 9/11 attacks, but critics argue that the prediction was too vague to have any practical meaning before the event occurred. They assert that this symbolic style allows for multiple interpretations, making it easy to mold her words to fit different outcomes retrospectively.

Another point of skepticism lies in the lack of documented evidence directly attributed to Baba Vanga. Much of what we know about her predictions comes from secondhand accounts, shared by people who visited her or from followers who have preserved her prophecies through oral tradition. This lack of direct documentation has led some to question the authenticity of her predictions. Critics argue that many of her prophecies may have been exaggerated or even fabricated over the years by followers eager to believe in her gifts. Without concrete documentation, it becomes challenging to separate Baba Vanga's original words from the interpretations and embellishments that may have been added later.

There is also the issue of the prophecies that did not come true. While some of Baba Vanga's predictions seem remarkably accurate, others have proven inaccurate or are still pending. For example, she reportedly predicted that Europe would cease to exist by the year 2016 due to a drastic population shift, a prophecy that did not come to pass. Skeptics point to such examples as evidence that her prophecies are unreliable and that her reputation may be more myth than reality. However, her supporters counter this by arguing that not all prophecies are set in stone and that her visions were meant to serve as warnings, offering humanity the chance to change its path.

Psychologists and skeptics also offer scientific explanations for Baba Vanga's predictions, suggesting that her "visions" were likely products of intuition or high empathy rather than supernatural foresight. Baba Vanga's sensitive nature, combined with her blindness, may have heightened her ability to read subtle emotional cues and patterns, allowing her to make educated guesses about people's lives and even world events. This phenomenon, known as "cold reading," is a skill that some psychologists believe may explain her apparent accuracy in personal readings. By tapping into the emotions, behaviors, and fears of the people around her, she could offer insights that resonated deeply with those who sought her counsel.

Another possible explanation from skeptics is the "Barnum Effect," a psychological phenomenon where people interpret vague or general statements as personally meaningful. For example, when Baba Vanga spoke in metaphors about upcoming disasters or transformations, listeners interpreted these messages as deeply relevant to their lives, even if they could apply to a broad range of situations. Skeptics argue that the Barnum Effect may explain why many people feel that her prophecies were accurate, as her predictions could be easily adapted to fit a variety of contexts.

Despite these skeptical arguments, there remains a core of devoted believers who see her prophecies as evidence of true clairvoyance. For them, Baba Vanga's accuracy in predicting specific global events is too compelling to ignore, and they view her as a rare figure who possessed genuine spiritual insight. Many believe that the mysteries surrounding her life and process only add to her credibility, emphasizing that the mystical cannot always be explained through science or logic. For these followers, Baba Vanga's prophecies are not just predictions but a moral and spiritual guide to navigating the uncertainties of the modern world.

Ultimately, Baba Vanga's prophecies sit at the crossroads of belief and doubt, inviting us to explore the boundaries between intuition, spirituality, and psychology. Her supporters are steadfast in their belief that she was a divinely gifted seer who could access knowledge beyond human understanding, while skeptics remain firm in their conviction that her abilities can be explained through natural means. This ongoing debate is part of her legacy, a testament to the mystery that surrounded her and the allure of prophecy itself.

For those who look to Baba Vanga's predictions for 2025 and beyond, her legacy serves as both an inspiration and a caution. Whether one views her prophecies as genuine visions of the future or as the imaginative insights of a perceptive mind, they challenge us to question the nature of foresight, the limits of human perception, and the mysteries of the unknown.

Global Perspectives on Prophecy and Predictions

Prophecy and the desire to foresee the future are not unique to any single culture or religion. Across the globe, the concept of prophecy holds a deeply rooted place in human history, with nearly every civilization developing its own methods, beliefs, and traditions surrounding the idea of predicting what lies ahead. From ancient oracles to modern mystics, humanity's quest to peer beyond the present moment reflects an enduring fascination with the unknown and a desire to gain insight into potential challenges and opportunities.

In ancient Greece, prophecy was institutionalized through the Oracle of Delphi, where priestesses, believed to be vessels of the god Apollo, provided cryptic answers to those seeking guidance. This tradition became a cornerstone of Greek society, with generals, politicians, and even kings consulting the oracle before making significant decisions. The Greeks viewed prophecy as a bridge between the divine and mortal realms, believing that the gods could reveal truths that lay beyond human understanding. Prophecies in Greek culture were often ambiguous, allowing for interpretation and adaptation as events unfolded. This adaptability is a common trait in prophecies across cultures, adding a layer of mystique to their meaning.

In ancient China, the practice of divination was equally integral to the culture. The I Ching, or Book of Changes, is one of the oldest divinatory texts in existence and is still consulted today. Through a system of hexagrams and symbolic interpretations, the I Ching offers insights into the cycles of life, providing guidance based on an individual's current situation. This method emphasizes harmony with natural forces, suggesting that the future is shaped not only by human actions but also by the rhythms and patterns of the universe. Chinese prophecy thus carries a philosophical dimension, teaching that understanding the flow of energy, or "qi," is key to anticipating what lies ahead.

In Mesoamerican civilizations like the Maya and Aztec cultures, prophecy took on a cosmic scale. The Maya developed complex calendars, such as the Long Count, which tracked vast cycles of time and marked important cosmological transitions. The end of one of these cycles in 2012 was famously misinterpreted as a prediction of the end of the world, yet in reality, it symbolized a renewal, a shift in cosmic energy rather than a literal end. For these cultures, prophecy was interwoven with astronomy and an understanding of time as cyclical, where major transitions were seen as opportunities for renewal and change rather than as fixed events.

The Abrahamic religions—Judaism, Christianity, and Islam—also place a strong emphasis on prophecy. In the Old Testament, prophets like Isaiah and Ezekiel warned of divine retribution, offering their followers guidance on living in alignment with God's will. Christian prophecy, especially in the New Testament's Book of Revelation, is known for its apocalyptic imagery and warnings of the final judgment. In Islam, prophecy is a central tenet, with Muhammad regarded as the final prophet. Islamic eschatology includes various prophecies about the end times, such as the arrival of the Mahdi and the return of Jesus. These prophecies emphasize moral behavior and preparation for ultimate judgment, reinforcing the idea that prophecy serves as a guide for ethical conduct and spiritual readiness.

In Hinduism, prophecy and prediction take the form of cyclical time periods called "yugas," or ages, with each age representing different qualities of human consciousness and social order. According to Hindu texts, humanity is currently in the Kali Yuga, the age of darkness and materialism, which will eventually give way to a new era of enlightenment. Hindu prophecies often highlight the transformative power of time, suggesting that every cycle brings forth a new opportunity for spiritual evolution. This cyclical view emphasizes resilience and the understanding that all things, including human society, are part of an eternal cycle of birth, death, and rebirth.

The indigenous cultures of North America also hold unique perspectives on prophecy, with traditions that focus on visions and spirit communication. Native American tribes, like the Hopi, have a rich prophetic tradition that includes warnings of environmental destruction and social decay. The Hopi prophecies, known for their symbolism and imagery, highlight the need for humanity to live in harmony with the earth. The Hopi view these warnings as lessons, suggesting that if humanity respects and protects nature, future catastrophes can be averted. For many indigenous cultures, prophecy is not merely about predicting events but is deeply connected to their worldview, where spiritual balance with the environment and respect for all forms of life are central to survival and prosperity.

In modern times, prophecy has expanded beyond traditional religious and cultural contexts to include scientific and economic predictions, often using data-driven models to forecast trends in climate, economy, and social behaviors. While these predictions are not mystical, they serve a similar function—guiding humanity's actions in the face of uncertainty. Climate scientists, for instance, provide projections about global warming's effects, offering humanity a chance to take preventative action. Economists predict recessions or booms based on historical data and economic indicators, helping governments and individuals make informed decisions about the future. Although these predictions differ from traditional prophecy, they fulfill the same desire: to foresee what lies ahead and prepare for it.

Despite the evolution of prophecy, common themes endure. In almost all global perspectives, prophecy involves a moral or ethical component, reminding people of their responsibilities to themselves, others, and the world. Prophecy, whether mystical or data-based, prompts us to reflect on our choices, urging us toward actions that promote balance, harmony, and survival. In this sense, prophecy acts as a mirror, revealing potential consequences of human behavior and encouraging self-examination.

Baba Vanga's prophecies, though situated within the cultural context of Eastern Europe, resonate with these global themes. Her visions are often moral in nature, warning against human hubris, environmental degradation, and unchecked technological advancement. While her followers see her as a distinctly Balkan figure, her prophecies align with universal messages found in other cultures and traditions. Like the Hopi warnings about environmental destruction or the Hindu understanding of cyclical ages, Baba Vanga's visions reflect an understanding that humanity's choices determine its destiny.

However, Baba Vanga's prophecies also highlight a unique fusion of mysticism and modern concerns, addressing issues such as artificial intelligence, genetic engineering, and the rise of superpowers. This blend of the ancient and modern gives her prophecies a distinctive relevance, showing that while prophecy has deep roots in tradition, it also evolves with the times. Baba Vanga's predictions for 2025 echo the same themes found in historical prophecies while addressing issues that reflect the anxieties and hopes of the contemporary world.

In exploring these global perspectives, it becomes clear that prophecy serves as a universal guide, a reminder that humanity's future is shaped by the choices made today. Baba Vanga, like prophets before her, offers insight into possible futures, encouraging individuals and societies to reflect on their actions and values. Her prophecies align with a global tapestry of foresight, where each culture contributes its own wisdom and cautionary tales, urging humanity to consider its impact on the world and to pursue a path that fosters harmony, justice, and respect.

As we delve further into Baba Vanga's predictions for the year 2025, we do so with an understanding that prophecy is more than mere prediction; it is a tradition that transcends time and place, a tool for introspection and a call to action. Through these global perspectives, we see that her prophecies are part of a larger human quest to find meaning, purpose, and guidance in a world full of uncertainty, drawing from the timeless need to connect with forces greater than ourselves.

What Do Prophecies Mean for Modern Society?

In a world increasingly driven by science, technology, and data, prophecy might seem like a relic of the past. Yet, the allure of prophecy endures, and interest in visions of the future remains robust even in modern society. Whether through the ancient words of Nostradamus, the teachings of indigenous shamans, or the cryptic predictions of mystics like Baba Vanga, prophecy continues to captivate, offering a blend of mystery, hope, and caution. But what do prophecies truly mean for today's world? What role do they play in an era where facts and evidence are highly prized? This chapter explores the multifaceted role of prophecy in modern society, delving into why humanity's fascination with foretelling the future remains strong and how these predictions intersect with contemporary issues.

In a practical sense, prophecies provide a lens through which people can process complex global events and uncertainties. Economic instability, environmental crises, political turmoil, and rapid technological advancements create a sense of unpredictability. Prophecies offer a framework for interpreting these developments, transforming random events into part of a larger story with meaning and purpose. Prophets like Baba Vanga are seen by some as guides, helping to explain these seemingly chaotic times and giving direction amid uncertainty. In this way, prophecies serve a psychological function, allowing people to find meaning in what might otherwise feel overwhelming or senseless.

Prophecy also fulfills a universal desire for hope and reassurance. For many, prophecies are not just warnings of potential dangers; they also carry messages of resilience and survival. In times of hardship or crisis, prophecies that foretell eventual triumph or redemption can inspire people to persevere. For instance, Baba Vanga's predictions about spiritual awakening and societal transformation resonate with those who hope that humanity's challenges can ultimately lead to positive change. This hopeful dimension of prophecy offers an emotional anchor, reinforcing the belief that humanity can overcome even its greatest obstacles.

Prophecies also encourage ethical reflection and moral responsibility, themes that resonate strongly with modern audiences. Many prophecies across cultures emphasize the importance of living in harmony with nature, treating others with respect, and avoiding hubris. These messages are especially pertinent today, as humanity faces ecological crises, social injustice, and ethical dilemmas surrounding technological advances. Baba Vanga's warnings against environmental degradation, unchecked technological ambition, and loss of spiritual values speak directly to issues that modern society grapples with. Her prophecies, like those from other traditions, urge people to consider the consequences of their actions, making them relevant reminders of the need for a more conscientious approach to progress.

In addition to ethical reflection, prophecies often serve as a critique of modern life, challenging the values and behaviors that dominate contemporary society. By warning of the potential dangers of over-reliance on technology, materialism, or environmental exploitation, prophets offer an alternative perspective to mainstream narratives.

Baba Vanga's visions of future challenges posed by artificial intelligence, global power struggles, and spiritual decline encourage individuals to rethink societal priorities. Her predictions suggest that pursuing progress without balance can lead to unintended consequences, encouraging society to re-evaluate what it values most.

Despite the ongoing fascination with prophecy, modern society also approaches it with a measure of skepticism. This skepticism is partly due to the scientific method's emphasis on empirical evidence, which contrasts sharply with the often symbolic and metaphorical nature of prophecies. Unlike scientific predictions, which are based on data and testable hypotheses, prophecies are typically based on intuition, spiritual insight, or divine revelation. For many, this makes prophecy appear subjective or unreliable, leading to a divide between those who believe in the power of prophecy and those who see it as an outdated or superstitious practice.

Yet, even among skeptics, there is an acknowledgment of prophecy's cultural and psychological impact. In a world where answers are often sought in data and technology, prophecy offers a reminder of humanity's innate desire to connect with forces beyond the material world. This yearning for transcendence persists, even as science advances, revealing that human nature is not easily satisfied by rationality alone. Prophecies provide a bridge between the tangible and intangible, blending ancient wisdom with modern aspirations, allowing people to engage with mysteries that lie beyond the scope of scientific understanding.

Prophecies also influence popular culture, demonstrating their enduring impact on the collective imagination. Movies, books, and television series often draw on prophetic themes, exploring scenarios of apocalyptic events, dystopian futures, or world-changing revelations. These stories, while fictional, tap into society's fascination with the unknown and the allure of foreknowledge. Prophetic narratives serve as both cautionary tales and sources of escapism, allowing audiences to engage with the concept of fate and destiny in a safe, controlled setting. The popularity of these themes reflects an ongoing cultural dialogue about the future, the unknown, and humanity's place in the cosmos.

For some, prophecy provides a counterbalance to modern society's emphasis on control and predictability. In a world where technology increasingly aims to minimize uncertainty, prophecies remind us that not everything can be controlled or predicted. Baba Vanga's predictions, for example, often touch on events that defy human planning or influence, underscoring the idea that some aspects of the future remain unknowable. This perspective can be humbling, reinforcing the notion that, despite our advancements, we are part of a larger, mysterious universe that operates according to its own rules.

Prophecies like Baba Vanga's also raise important questions about free will versus destiny. Her predictions about future events suggest a certain inevitability, yet her warnings imply that humanity has the power to influence outcomes. This tension between fate and choice resonates deeply with contemporary audiences, who are often caught between a desire for security and a belief in self-determination. In this sense, prophecies invite individuals to consider their role in shaping the future, empowering them to take responsibility for their actions while remaining open to forces beyond their control.

Furthermore, prophecy in modern society invites an exploration of spiritual and philosophical beliefs. For many, predictions like those of Baba Vanga reflect a worldview that acknowledges unseen forces or spiritual dimensions, challenging the purely materialistic view of existence. This perspective resonates with those seeking a deeper understanding of life, purpose, and interconnectedness. Prophecies allow individuals to engage with existential questions, offering a sense of continuity and connection across time and space.

In examining what prophecies mean for modern society, it becomes clear that they are more than predictions—they are reflections of humanity's deepest fears, hopes, and desires. Whether people believe in prophecy or not, its presence in the modern world invites reflection, ethical introspection, and a sense of wonder. Baba Vanga's predictions for the year 2025, for example, serve as a mirror for today's challenges, encouraging society to consider its values, priorities, and responsibilities. Her prophecies underscore the idea that the future is shaped not only by external events but by the choices, beliefs, and actions of individuals and communities.

Ultimately, prophecies in modern society represent a fusion of ancient wisdom and contemporary concerns, a bridge that connects the past, present, and future. They serve as both cautionary tales and sources of hope, reminding humanity that while the future may be uncertain, it is also filled with possibilities. In Baba Vanga's prophecies and the prophecies of others, modern society finds not only glimpses of potential outcomes but also an invitation to engage with the unknown, to approach the future with both humility and hope, and to consider the profound impact of our actions on the world yet to come.

The Relevance of Prophecy in Today's World Affairs

As global crises intensify, the relevance of prophecy has gained new prominence, with people turning to ancient predictions and modern prophets to find meaning and direction. In an age defined by political tension, environmental challenges, and rapid technological advancement, prophecy offers a unique lens through which people interpret unfolding events, understand deeper patterns, and seek guidance. Figures like Baba Vanga, who foresaw global upheavals and warned of humanity's potential self-destruction, resonate strongly today, as her predictions mirror issues currently facing society. In this chapter, we'll examine how prophecy intersects with today's world affairs, offering insights and lessons amid modern complexity.

In today's political landscape, many find a sense of guidance and even cautionary warning in prophecy. Baba Vanga's predictions, for instance, spoke of shifting power dynamics, rising conflicts, and the potential for new alliances, themes that resonate in a world increasingly polarized by ideological, economic, and territorial disputes. Her visions align with the anxieties people feel regarding global instability and the potential for large-scale conflict. Some interpret her predictions as a call for diplomatic solutions and global unity, warning that unchecked aggression and greed could lead to devastating consequences. In this sense, her prophecies serve as both a mirror to current challenges and a reminder of the need for mindful, ethical leadership.

Beyond politics, Baba Vanga's prophecies around environmental crises are especially relevant as humanity faces unprecedented ecological challenges. She foresaw climate disasters, describing changes in weather patterns, catastrophic floods, and droughts, predictions that are eerily aligned with the realities of climate change today. Her visions warned of "rivers changing their course" and "oceans swallowing the land," metaphorical language that aligns closely with rising sea levels, melting glaciers, and increased natural disasters like hurricanes and wildfires. For many, her environmental prophecies emphasize the need for urgent action, encouraging a shift in how we relate to the planet. They serve as a powerful reminder that human survival depends on environmental stewardship and respect for natural limits.

Prophecies are also relevant in today's discussions about technology. Baba Vanga foresaw rapid advancements that would transform society but also warned of the ethical dilemmas they could create. Her predictions on artificial intelligence, genetic engineering, and other scientific breakthroughs mirror contemporary debates about the risks and rewards of technology. For instance, as AI and biotechnology advance, questions arise about privacy, the ethics of genetic manipulation, and the long-term consequences of delegating decision-making to machines. Baba Vanga's prophecies reflect the concerns many feel about these advancements, warning that technology, if not balanced with ethics, could lead to societal and existential threats. Her foresight serves as a reminder of the importance of approaching innovation with caution, mindfulness, and an ethical framework.

Moreover, Baba Vanga's prophecies on spiritual and social awakening resonate with a growing global movement toward self-reflection and a search for meaning. In her visions, she spoke of a time when humanity would re-evaluate its values, turn inward, and seek higher understanding amid external chaos. Today, more people are turning to meditation, mindfulness practices, and spiritual traditions to find grounding in an uncertain world. Her predictions of a global "spiritual awakening" mirror the societal shift towards mental well-being, personal growth, and an emphasis on interconnectedness. For many, this awakening is seen as a necessary counterbalance to the materialism and technological dominance of modern life, encouraging humanity to reconnect with values that promote compassion, unity, and peace.

Prophecy, particularly Baba Vanga's, has also become increasingly relevant in discussions about globalization and cultural convergence. In a world where countries and cultures are interconnected in unprecedented ways, her predictions about a global community facing shared challenges are strikingly prescient. Issues like pandemics, economic instability, and resource scarcity highlight the importance of global cooperation. Her prophecies suggest that humanity's survival may depend on collective action and a move away from divisive ideologies. For many, her visions serve as a reminder that the fate of individual nations is intertwined with the well-being of the entire planet, emphasizing the need for mutual respect, collaboration, and empathy across borders.

Prophecies also hold a special relevance in times of public health crises. Baba Vanga reportedly foresaw the spread of pandemics, hinting at waves of illness that would impact humanity on a large scale. Her warnings about health challenges have been revisited amid recent global health issues, prompting people to consider the possibility of more frequent outbreaks as population density increases and environmental changes make viral transmissions more likely. Baba Vanga's predictions serve as a stark reminder of the importance of preparedness, scientific research, and a cooperative approach to healthcare. Her foresight in this area reinforces the need for international collaboration to prevent and manage future crises effectively.

One reason prophecy remains relevant in today's world affairs is its ability to address the interconnectedness of complex global issues. Prophecies like Baba Vanga's do not isolate political, environmental, technological, or spiritual concerns but view them as parts of an integrated whole. Her predictions suggest that disruptions in one area can create ripple effects across others, a perspective increasingly recognized in contemporary analyses of global challenges. For example, climate change impacts food security, which in turn affects economic stability and political tensions. Her prophecies encourage a holistic view of world affairs, highlighting the importance of comprehensive solutions that address underlying causes rather than merely treating symptoms.

Baba Vanga's prophecies also resonate because they present a moral dimension, urging humanity to consider the ethical implications of its choices. Her warnings about environmental neglect, technological hubris, and the potential for societal division reflect a concern for the values that underpin human actions. In today's world, where economic profit and rapid progress often overshadow ethical considerations, her prophecies challenge societies to think deeply about what they prioritize. They urge leaders and individuals alike to reflect on their responsibilities to each other and to future generations, emphasizing the need for wisdom, humility, and foresight.

Another dimension of prophecy's relevance is its role in offering hope and motivation. In a world beset by constant news of crises, prophecies like Baba Vanga's serve as reminders that humanity can choose a different path. Her visions of spiritual awakening, social progress, and unity inspire people to work towards positive change, even in difficult times. For many, these prophecies are not fixed predictions but calls to action, suggesting that humanity has the power to influence the future through mindful and responsible choices. This perspective transforms prophecy from a passive forecast into an active encouragement to shape a better world.

The continued relevance of prophecy in world affairs also lies in its symbolic power, as it transcends cultural, religious, and linguistic barriers. Prophets like Baba Vanga embody universal concerns—survival, justice, peace, and harmony—while resonating with the unique hopes and fears of different societies. Her predictions serve as a common language for discussing humanity's shared future, bridging gaps and inspiring conversations that might otherwise be difficult to initiate. In this way, prophecy becomes a unifying force, inviting people from diverse backgrounds to reflect on the challenges and possibilities that lie ahead.

In examining the relevance of prophecy in today's world, it becomes evident that figures like Baba Vanga offer more than mystical predictions; they provide a framework for understanding and responding to complex modern issues. Her prophecies on environmental, political, technological, and social topics address key concerns in world affairs, reminding humanity of the stakes at play and encouraging a more mindful approach to the future. By blending caution with hope, her visions invite people to reflect on their actions, embrace ethical responsibility, and work toward a future marked by balance and harmony.

As we continue to explore Baba Vanga's specific predictions for the year 2025, it is clear that prophecy holds a unique place in modern society, where ancient wisdom and contemporary challenges intersect. Prophecy remains relevant not only as a tool for understanding the world but as a reminder that the future is not merely something to be awaited—it is something to be shaped. Through the wisdom embedded in prophecy, humanity is reminded of its capacity to navigate uncertainty, make thoughtful choices, and create a world aligned with its highest ideals.

A First Look at 2025: Key Predictions and Their Themes

The year 2025 is pivotal in Baba Vanga's visions—a year marked by profound change, potential upheaval, and significant transformation. Her predictions for this year span a wide array of themes, from environmental disasters and political realignments to technological breakthroughs and spiritual awakenings. These themes echo many concerns that resonate deeply today, offering both caution and insight into the future humanity may face. As we delve into her prophecies for 2025, certain core themes emerge, each one reflecting an area of modern life undergoing rapid transformation and facing considerable challenges.

One of the foremost themes in Baba Vanga's predictions for 2025 is **environmental upheaval**. Her visions are rife with imagery of floods, storms, droughts, and other natural disasters, highlighting her concern for the planet's ecological stability. Baba Vanga warned that human disregard for nature would lead to extreme environmental consequences, and she saw 2025 as a year when these effects would become undeniable. Her predictions spoke of "oceans rising" and "land being reclaimed by water," metaphors that seem to align with current concerns over rising sea levels, deforestation, and climate-induced disasters. For many, her environmental warnings are a call to action, urging humanity to adopt sustainable practices and work to preserve the delicate balance of nature.

Another recurring theme in her predictions is **technological advancement and its ethical dilemmas**. Baba Vanga foresaw major breakthroughs in artificial intelligence, genetic engineering, and biotechnology, developments that could transform human life in unprecedented ways. However, she also warned of the potential consequences if these advancements were pursued without ethical considerations. Her visions included references to machines taking over certain human tasks and the merging of biology and technology, which can be interpreted as predictions about AI's growing role in society and advancements in bioengineering. Baba Vanga's prophecies suggest that while technology holds great promise, it also poses risks to human autonomy, identity, and ethics. In 2025, society may face critical choices about how to integrate these advancements responsibly.

Closely tied to technological themes is her prediction of **a shift in global power dynamics**. Baba Vanga foresaw significant changes in international relations, with new alliances forming and old ones breaking apart. She spoke of a "realignment" among nations, where emerging powers would challenge established ones, reshaping the balance of global influence. This theme resonates with current geopolitical tensions and the rise of countries that are rapidly gaining economic and political influence. Her predictions for 2025 indicate a world on the brink of a new order, where cooperation and competition coexist in unpredictable ways. Her followers interpret these prophecies as a warning to prepare for diplomatic shifts that could either foster global unity or deepen divisions.

Alongside these shifts, Baba Vanga predicted a period of **social unrest and collective questioning**. She saw 2025 as a time when societies would grapple with issues of inequality, justice, and the distribution of resources. Her visions included images of protests, social movements, and a demand for reform, suggesting that people would increasingly call for accountability from their leaders. This theme aligns with ongoing struggles for human rights, economic equity, and political transparency across the world. Baba Vanga's prophecies indicate that in 2025, these demands may reach a boiling point, compelling societies to address longstanding issues of inequality and work towards fairer systems.

In contrast to these warnings, Baba Vanga's predictions for 2025 also carry a theme of **spiritual awakening and renewal**. Amid the challenges she foresaw, she also predicted a shift in human consciousness—a desire for deeper meaning, connection, and understanding. This awakening, according to her visions, would not be limited to individual self-discovery but would reflect a collective movement toward higher values and spiritual growth. She saw people increasingly questioning materialism, seeking inner peace, and turning towards practices that foster mindfulness and compassion. This spiritual renaissance is a hopeful theme within her prophecies, suggesting that the trials of 2025 could inspire humanity to adopt values that transcend material concerns.

Another fascinating theme in Baba Vanga's prophecies for 2025 is the potential for **new discoveries in space** and even **interplanetary communication**. She believed that humanity's interest in exploring the cosmos would intensify, driven by scientific curiosity and the search for extraterrestrial life. Her visions included hints of potential contact or breakthroughs in understanding the universe beyond Earth. While some view this as a metaphor for humanity's desire to expand its horizons, others see it as a literal prediction of space exploration milestones. With contemporary advancements in space technology and growing interest in missions to Mars and beyond, this theme aligns with humanity's deepening engagement with the cosmos.

Baba Vanga's prophecies for 2025 also touch on **public health challenges**, foreseeing an era where humanity faces new illnesses and health crises. She spoke of diseases that would challenge current medical knowledge, potentially leading to global efforts to innovate and find solutions. This theme is particularly relevant given recent health crises, and her predictions suggest that in 2025, humanity might face another test of its resilience and capacity for cooperation in the face of health threats. Her prophecies emphasize the importance of preparation, research, and collaboration, highlighting the need for robust healthcare systems that can respond to emerging challenges.

The final theme in her predictions for 2025 is the notion of a **collective reckoning and the power of choice**. Baba Vanga believed that this year would be a crossroads, a time when humanity would be forced to confront the consequences of its actions and make critical decisions about its future. Whether addressing environmental, technological, or social issues, her prophecies consistently return to the idea that humanity's destiny depends on its choices. She envisioned 2025 as a year when humanity would either rise to meet its challenges or risk losing control over its own fate. This sense of urgency serves as a reminder that the future is not predetermined but shaped by the choices of individuals, communities, and nations.

In looking at these key themes, it becomes clear that Baba Vanga's predictions for 2025 are both cautionary and inspirational. They reflect a deep understanding of the interconnected nature of modern issues, highlighting how changes in one area can ripple across others. Her prophecies underscore the complexity of contemporary life, where advancements and challenges are woven together in ways that require careful consideration and mindful action.

For many, Baba Vanga's predictions are a reminder that humanity stands at a critical juncture—a time when choices about the environment, technology, politics, and social values will shape the world for generations to come. Her visions encourage reflection on the path society is taking, inspiring individuals and leaders alike to act with wisdom, responsibility, and compassion.

As we proceed to examine each of these themes in detail throughout this book, we'll see how Baba Vanga's prophecies continue to resonate with the realities of today. Whether viewed as literal predictions or allegorical insights, her visions offer a profound look into the challenges and possibilities of 2025, urging humanity to confront its greatest trials with courage, integrity, and a commitment to positive transformation.

Natural Disasters Foretold for 2025

Among Baba Vanga's most striking predictions for 2025 are her visions of natural disasters—cataclysmic events that would disrupt regions, reshape landscapes, and challenge the resilience of societies across the world. In her prophecies, she described a series of environmental calamities that would serve as both a warning and a consequence of humanity's actions. These foreseen disasters are depicted as a powerful reminder of nature's immense force and humanity's vulnerability in the face of ecological upheaval. This chapter explores the types of natural disasters Baba Vanga predicted for 2025, examining the possible significance of each and how they might connect to current environmental trends.

One of the most prominent natural disasters she foretold for 2025 involves **flooding on an unprecedented scale**. Baba Vanga described images of water engulfing coastal cities, rivers overflowing their banks, and entire communities submerged. She warned of rising sea levels that would reclaim portions of coastal lands, displacing populations and sparking migration crises. For her followers, this prophecy aligns closely with the warnings issued by climate scientists today, who predict that rising global temperatures will lead to accelerated polar ice melt, causing sea levels to rise. Low-lying areas, from small island nations to major urban centers, face heightened risks of flooding, reinforcing Baba Vanga's vision of a world grappling with the repercussions of unchecked climate change.

In addition to floods, Baba Vanga also foresaw **violent storms and extreme weather patterns** that would bring destruction to numerous regions. She described storms of unusual strength and frequency, with hurricane-force winds, torrential rains, and devastating impacts on communities in their paths. Her vision includes hurricanes, typhoons, and cyclones that would grow in power due to the warming of ocean waters, a phenomenon well-documented by climate experts. The intensity of these storms is already on the rise, as warmer oceans provide more energy to fuel them. Her predictions suggest that 2025 could be a year of heightened storm activity, challenging infrastructure, resilience, and emergency preparedness in affected areas.

Another natural disaster Baba Vanga predicted for 2025 involves **earthquakes** in regions typically seen as stable. She described visions of land trembling, cities collapsing, and landscapes shifting dramatically, hinting at powerful seismic events that would affect areas unaccustomed to such disturbances. This prediction raises concerns, as tectonic activity in traditionally stable areas could catch populations off guard, resulting in severe consequences. Baba Vanga's prophecy speaks to the unpredictable nature of seismic activity and serves as a reminder that even seemingly stable areas can face sudden geological upheaval. Her followers interpret this prediction as a warning to remain vigilant and to invest in infrastructure that can withstand such shocks, regardless of location.

Closely related to her predictions of earthquakes, Baba Vanga also foresaw **volcanic eruptions** with far-reaching effects. Her visions included images of fiery mountains spewing ash and lava, covering entire areas in darkness and disrupting life far beyond their immediate vicinity. She warned of volcanic eruptions that could impact global air quality, agriculture, and climate, as volcanic ash and gases could temporarily cool the atmosphere.

The potential for eruptions to impact regions thousands of miles away speaks to the interconnectedness of natural systems and the far-reaching effects of such events. Some of her followers interpret these visions as a call to pay closer attention to active volcanoes and to develop strategies for mitigating the impact of large eruptions on both local and global scales.

Baba Vanga's prophecy for 2025 also includes **droughts** and **wildfires**, which she described as a "scorching of the land" that would render areas uninhabitable. She envisioned barren fields, water sources drying up, and wildfires sweeping across landscapes with fierce intensity. This prediction aligns with recent trends of increasingly severe droughts, especially in regions already vulnerable to water scarcity. As temperatures rise, many areas are experiencing prolonged dry spells that reduce water availability and create ideal conditions for wildfires. Baba Vanga's visions suggest that in 2025, droughts and fires may reach new levels of severity, impacting food security, displacing people, and straining resources.

Additionally, Baba Vanga foresaw **ice-related disasters** in unexpected locations. She described scenes of intense cold and snowfall hitting regions unaccustomed to such conditions, leading to disruptions in transportation, power outages, and widespread challenges for affected communities. With climate change contributing to unpredictable weather patterns, phenomena like polar vortex events have brought record-low temperatures to places that rarely experience extreme cold. Her predictions about ice-related disasters highlight the growing instability in global weather patterns and suggest that unusual cold spells could become more frequent, bringing with them new hazards for regions ill-prepared for such extremes.

Beyond these specific events, Baba Vanga also spoke of **widespread ecological imbalances**, which she believed would destabilize entire ecosystems and disrupt human life. She warned of mass die-offs in wildlife, the spread of invasive species, and cascading effects that would impact food chains and biodiversity. These visions align with modern concerns about biodiversity loss, habitat destruction, and the destabilizing effects of human activity on natural systems. Her followers interpret these ecological warnings as a reminder that humanity's well-being is inextricably linked to the health of the environment and that ignoring these signs could lead to irreversible consequences.

The thread that ties all of Baba Vanga's predictions about natural disasters together is her underlying message about humanity's relationship with nature. She believed that these disasters would not occur randomly but would be a response to humanity's disregard for the environment. Her visions serve as a warning of the potential consequences of ecological neglect and the urgent need for change. Baba Vanga's prophecies for 2025 suggest that these disasters could serve as wake-up calls, encouraging people to rethink their treatment of the planet and to adopt more sustainable practices.

For many, Baba Vanga's predictions about natural disasters in 2025 are a reminder of the power of nature and humanity's limited control over it. In an era marked by rapid industrialization, resource extraction, and environmental degradation, her visions invite people to reconsider the long-term impacts of their actions.

These disasters are not merely warnings of suffering but are seen by her followers as opportunities to recalibrate humanity's relationship with the Earth. They inspire reflection on the importance of environmental stewardship, the need for resilience, and the significance of proactive adaptation to a changing world.

As we look ahead to 2025, Baba Vanga's predictions challenge us to confront the realities of climate change, natural disasters, and ecological instability with a sense of urgency and responsibility. Her visions call for greater awareness of how human actions shape the environment, urging societies to invest in sustainable practices, disaster preparedness, and global cooperation. In doing so, we can mitigate the effects of these natural disasters and perhaps even prevent some of the devastation she foresaw.

In the coming chapters, we will explore further predictions for 2025, each one offering additional insights into the themes of change, challenge, and transformation that Baba Vanga believed would define this year. Her visions of natural disasters serve as a powerful reminder that while humanity may wield tremendous power, it remains a part of a larger, complex system that demands respect, responsibility, and humility.

Environmental Challenges and Climate Crisis in 2025

Baba Vanga's predictions for 2025 emphasize environmental challenges as a central theme, reflecting her deep concerns about humanity's treatment of the planet and the far-reaching consequences of ecological neglect. She foresaw a world grappling with severe climate-related crises that would impact not only nature but also every facet of human life. Her visions depict 2025 as a year when the effects of climate change would become undeniable, demanding urgent action and a fundamental shift in humanity's approach to the environment. In this chapter, we explore her predictions on the climate crisis and environmental challenges, as well as their resonance with current ecological issues.

A primary aspect of Baba Vanga's environmental prophecies involves **extreme weather events** that would disrupt the natural balance and pose significant risks to human societies. She spoke of unusual heatwaves, prolonged droughts, and unexpected cold spells—all contributing to increased instability. Her visions align with scientific predictions regarding climate change, which has intensified weather extremes across the globe. According to climate scientists, global warming increases the likelihood of severe weather patterns, as rising temperatures contribute to hotter summers, harsher winters, and unpredictable storms. Baba Vanga's prophecies for 2025 suggest that these extremes would push societies to confront the reality of a changing climate and adapt to its impacts with more urgency than ever before.

Water scarcity was another critical issue in Baba Vanga's visions, as she foresaw widespread droughts and dwindling water resources affecting entire regions. She predicted that in 2025, water scarcity would emerge as one of humanity's most pressing challenges, leading to social unrest, economic struggles, and even migration crises. Her prophecy highlights a concern shared by environmental experts today: as temperatures rise and precipitation patterns change, many areas are expected to experience reduced water availability, particularly in already arid and semi-arid regions. Her followers interpret her visions of water scarcity as a warning to invest in sustainable water management practices, encourage conservation, and work toward equitable access to water—a resource she viewed as both precious and finite.

Closely tied to water scarcity is the issue of **food security**, which Baba Vanga foresaw as increasingly compromised by environmental degradation. She envisioned 2025 as a year marked by agricultural challenges, with failed crops, soil depletion, and difficulties in food production becoming common. This theme is especially relevant given today's concerns about the impact of climate change on agriculture. Rising temperatures, droughts, and extreme weather events are already affecting crop yields, threatening the stability of food supplies worldwide. Her prophecy serves as a reminder that food security is intricately connected to environmental health and that unsustainable farming practices and overexploitation of resources could lead to scarcity and hunger.

In addition to resource scarcity, Baba Vanga warned of **rising sea levels** and the threats they posed to coastal communities. She foresaw entire regions being submerged, forcing mass relocations and creating what we now refer to as "climate refugees." The melting of polar ice and the thermal expansion of seawater due to global warming have already led to rising sea levels, and this trend is expected to continue. In low-lying areas, such as island nations and coastal cities, this could result in the displacement of millions of people. Baba Vanga's vision of submerged lands and population displacement is a call to prepare for these impacts, urging policymakers and communities to consider coastal protection measures and relocation plans to ensure the safety and well-being of affected populations.

Another aspect of Baba Vanga's predictions relates to **biodiversity loss and ecosystem collapse**. She foresaw a decline in animal populations, the destruction of natural habitats, and a weakened biodiversity base, which would impact human life in unforeseen ways. In her view, 2025 would be a year when humanity would feel the consequences of the ongoing loss of plant and animal species, driven by deforestation, pollution, and climate change. Scientists agree that biodiversity loss is a critical issue, as ecosystems rely on a variety of species to maintain balance and support life. Baba Vanga's warnings about species decline and ecosystem disruption serve as a reminder of humanity's reliance on biodiversity for essentials like food, medicine, and clean air, emphasizing the need to protect and restore natural habitats.

A recurring theme in her visions was **the spread of pollution** and its impact on human health and the environment. Baba Vanga described images of contaminated rivers, polluted air, and degraded landscapes, foreseeing a world where industrial activity and consumerism would take a severe toll on natural resources. Her followers see this as a warning about the pervasive effects of pollution, which contribute not only to environmental harm but also to public health issues. In recent years, scientists have documented the adverse effects of air and water pollution on human health, with pollutants linked to respiratory diseases, cancers, and other illnesses. Baba Vanga's visions imply that by 2025, the consequences of pollution would be too severe to ignore, pushing humanity to implement stricter regulations and cleaner practices.

Baba Vanga's prophecy also touched on **deforestation and habitat destruction** as significant contributors to environmental instability. She foresaw vast tracts of forested land being cleared, leaving barren landscapes vulnerable to erosion, desertification, and loss of biodiversity. This prediction is particularly resonant today, as deforestation rates in regions like the Amazon and Southeast Asia continue to rise, driven by agriculture, logging, and urban expansion. Forests play a crucial role in absorbing carbon dioxide, maintaining soil health, and providing habitats for countless species. Her warnings suggest that if humanity continues to destroy forests at current rates, the resulting environmental imbalance could be catastrophic, leading to a cascade of problems for ecosystems and human societies alike.

Amid these dire warnings, Baba Vanga also offered glimpses of **human resilience and the potential for recovery** if proactive measures were taken. She believed that while the climate crisis posed immense challenges, it also presented an opportunity for transformation. In her view, 2025 could be a turning point, a year when societies recognize the need to fundamentally rethink their relationship with the environment. Baba Vanga envisioned humanity embracing sustainable technologies, renewable energy sources, and eco-friendly practices as part of a collective effort to address the climate crisis. This potential for recovery, she suggested, depended on humanity's willingness to adopt a more respectful and balanced approach to the natural world.

For her followers, Baba Vanga's environmental prophecies serve not only as a warning but as a call to action. Her visions underscore the interconnectedness of human life and the environment, reminding people that the consequences of environmental neglect are not isolated events but part of a larger, cumulative impact. The climate crisis, in her view, is a reflection of humanity's choices, and reversing its effects requires a commitment to restoring harmony with the Earth. Her prophecies encourage individuals, communities, and nations to adopt sustainable practices, reduce pollution, and protect natural resources as vital steps toward ensuring a habitable future.

In analyzing Baba Vanga's predictions for 2025, it is clear that environmental challenges are at the forefront of her vision. From extreme weather and resource scarcity to biodiversity loss and pollution, her prophecies highlight issues that require urgent attention and coordinated action. As the climate crisis becomes more pressing, her predictions offer insights into the potential consequences of inaction and the rewards of proactive measures.

The environmental challenges foreseen by Baba Vanga reflect a timeless truth about the delicate balance of life on Earth. Her visions remind us that humanity's future depends on its ability to recognize and respect this balance, to take responsibility for the impact of its actions, and to work toward a sustainable coexistence with nature. As we face the coming years, Baba Vanga's prophecies serve as both a caution and an inspiration—a call to protect the planet and ensure that future generations inherit a world where nature and humanity can thrive together.

The Shifting Poles: Is a Geomagnetic Flip Coming?

One of Baba Vanga's more enigmatic predictions for 2025 touches on the possibility of geomagnetic shifts, a phenomenon in which Earth's magnetic poles could "flip," reversing north and south. While such a reversal may sound like science fiction, geomagnetic pole shifts are a natural part of Earth's geological history and have occurred numerous times over millions of years. Baba Vanga's prophecy hints at a geomagnetic flip as a significant event in the near future, one that could have profound implications for the environment, technology, and human society. In this chapter, we explore what a geomagnetic flip entails, the scientific basis behind this possibility, and the potential consequences of such an event.

A **geomagnetic flip**, or pole reversal, occurs when Earth's magnetic field weakens, allowing the north and south magnetic poles to switch places. Geologists know that such reversals have happened before, with the last one, called the Brunhes-Matuyama reversal, occurring approximately 780,000 years ago. Although geomagnetic flips are rare, scientific evidence from sediment and volcanic rock records indicates that they are part of Earth's natural cycles. Some researchers believe we may be overdue for a flip, as data suggest that Earth's magnetic field has been gradually weakening over the past few centuries.

Baba Vanga's vision of a geomagnetic shift aligns with the concerns of some scientists who have observed changes in the magnetic field's strength and location. The North Magnetic Pole, for instance, has been moving at an accelerated pace over the past few decades, shifting from Canada toward Russia at an unprecedented rate. This unusual movement has sparked interest among geophysicists, who wonder whether it could be a precursor to a full pole reversal. Though these shifts don't confirm an impending flip, they highlight the fluid nature of Earth's magnetic field and the potential for future changes.

The potential consequences of a geomagnetic flip are complex and could affect various aspects of life on Earth. One of the most immediate impacts of a magnetic reversal would be on **navigation systems**, which rely on magnetic compasses to determine direction. In the event of a reversal, navigation systems worldwide would need recalibration to account for the flipped poles, which could lead to temporary confusion and disruptions, particularly in industries like aviation and maritime navigation. Modern GPS technology might mitigate some of these issues, but a magnetic flip could still challenge conventional navigation methods.

One of the more concerning implications of a geomagnetic flip is its potential effect on **Earth's protective magnetic shield**, which safeguards the planet from harmful solar and cosmic radiation. During a pole reversal, the magnetic field may weaken significantly, reducing Earth's natural defenses against these high-energy particles. This weakened magnetic field could increase the radiation exposure at Earth's surface, potentially affecting human health, disrupting ecosystems, and even damaging electronic infrastructure. Increased exposure to cosmic radiation could lead to higher incidences of radiation-related health issues, particularly for individuals in high-altitude regions or those frequently flying in airplanes.

In addition to health effects, a weakened magnetic field during a geomagnetic flip could pose risks to **satellite operations and power grids**. Satellite technology is especially vulnerable to space weather phenomena, such as solar flares and cosmic rays, which could increase in intensity if Earth's magnetic shield is weakened. Satellites play a crucial role in modern communication, navigation, and surveillance, and any disruption could have cascading effects across multiple sectors, from telecommunications to national security. Power grids could also be impacted, as geomagnetic storms could induce electrical currents that damage transformers and disrupt electricity distribution. Baba Vanga's prophecy of a geomagnetic shift, if it were to occur, could therefore foreshadow widespread technological challenges.

Baba Vanga's predictions about a potential geomagnetic shift also resonate with themes of **environmental change and ecological disruption**. The Earth's magnetic field interacts with atmospheric and oceanic currents, and while scientists are still studying the specifics, it is believed that a geomagnetic flip could potentially affect climate patterns. Some researchers speculate that changes in magnetic field strength could alter ocean circulation, leading to shifts in weather patterns and possibly intensifying certain climate phenomena. While this idea remains speculative, Baba Vanga's prophecy highlights the possibility that such a shift could have far-reaching environmental consequences.

One intriguing aspect of Baba Vanga's prophecy is the symbolic and metaphorical interpretation of a geomagnetic flip. Some followers interpret her vision as a metaphor for a "global shift" in human consciousness—a reversal not just of poles but of perspectives, priorities, and values. This interpretation suggests that the geomagnetic flip is a reflection of humanity's own potential to undergo transformation. As the poles change, so might humanity find itself at a crossroads, with a chance to redefine its relationship with the Earth, technology, and each other. In this sense, Baba Vanga's prophecy serves not only as a prediction of physical change but also as a call for inner transformation and balance.

A pole reversal, if it were to occur, would also challenge the adaptability and resilience of human civilization. History has shown that humanity is resourceful in the face of environmental challenges, but a geomagnetic flip would require cooperation, innovation, and preparation. Scientists are actively studying Earth's magnetic field to understand the risks and develop strategies for minimizing disruption, particularly in sectors reliant on magnetic orientation and electrical infrastructure. Preparing for the potential impacts of a geomagnetic shift could help mitigate some of the more serious consequences, demonstrating humanity's ability to adapt to even the most profound planetary changes.

Baba Vanga's prediction about a geomagnetic flip brings attention to the broader theme of **planetary resilience** and humanity's role in protecting and sustaining life on Earth. If her prophecy serves as a warning, it reminds us of the importance of understanding our planet's natural systems, respecting its cycles, and preparing for events beyond our immediate control. The Earth's magnetic field is a testament to the dynamic forces that sustain life, and its potential shifts highlight the interconnectedness of all things. Whether or not a geomagnetic flip happens in 2025, Baba Vanga's prophecy encourages a perspective of humility and awareness of the fragile systems that support life on Earth.

Baba Vanga's vision of a geomagnetic shift also invites us to explore humanity's relationship with cosmic forces. The magnetic field, though invisible, is a powerful reminder of Earth's connection to the broader universe, a shield that protects us from the constant flow of cosmic particles. The possibility of a pole reversal serves as a humbling reminder that, despite technological advancements, humanity remains subject to forces far beyond its control. Baba Vanga's prophecy calls us to recognize these cosmic connections and to approach our role on Earth with respect, foresight, and reverence.

In examining the potential for a geomagnetic flip and the implications of Baba Vanga's prophecy, we see that her vision goes beyond physical changes; it offers a perspective on resilience, adaptability, and consciousness. Whether interpreted as a literal forecast of a magnetic reversal or as a metaphor for a global shift, her prophecy challenges us to think about how we prepare for and respond to fundamental changes in our world.

As we continue to explore her predictions for 2025, the possibility of a geomagnetic shift serves as a powerful reminder of the unpredictable forces that shape our planet and our lives. It invites us to confront the unknown with curiosity and courage, to consider how we can strengthen our societies against potential disruptions, and to remember that change—whether physical, environmental, or spiritual—is a constant force in the universe.

Baba Vanga's Vision of Earthquakes and Volcanic Eruptions

Among Baba Vanga's vivid predictions for 2025 are her visions of earthquakes and volcanic eruptions that would shake the planet, bringing devastation to both familiar seismic zones and unexpected locations. She foresaw a year marked by powerful geological events, with tremors and eruptions serving as stark reminders of Earth's restless nature. In this chapter, we explore her prophecies surrounding earthquakes and volcanic eruptions, examining how they align with current scientific understanding and what they may signify about humanity's relationship with the natural world.

Baba Vanga described scenes of **earthquakes occurring in regions typically seen as seismically stable**, disrupting cities and unsettling communities unaccustomed to such forces. While most people expect earthquakes in certain "ring of fire" zones—regions where tectonic plates meet and interact—Baba Vanga's vision suggests that 2025 might see seismic activity in areas previously considered low-risk. This prediction resonates with recent geological findings that fault lines and pressure points exist in unexpected places, and dormant faults could be reactivated due to various geological pressures.

Some researchers argue that human activities like fracking and large-scale mining can induce earthquakes, potentially in regions that aren't historically prone to seismic activity. If Baba Vanga's prediction holds, it could mean a year where human actions inadvertently trigger geological instability, serving as a sobering reminder of the complex ways in which human activity impacts natural systems. Her prophecy suggests that even in seemingly stable locations, the Earth's crust remains dynamic and unpredictable, urging preparedness and awareness across broader areas.

In addition to earthquakes, Baba Vanga foresaw **catastrophic volcanic eruptions** affecting multiple regions. She spoke of mountains "spewing fire and ash," causing disruptions that would be felt far beyond the immediate areas. This vision includes not only the potential for destruction near volcanic sites but also the far-reaching effects of ash clouds, air quality degradation, and climate disruption. Volcanic eruptions can release massive quantities of ash and sulfur dioxide into the atmosphere, which, if large enough, can temporarily cool global temperatures by blocking sunlight. Baba Vanga's prophecy highlights the possibility that 2025 could bring such an eruption, affecting agriculture, weather patterns, and daily life on a global scale.

A notable aspect of her prophecy is the potential impact of a supervolcanic eruption, a rare but extremely powerful type of eruption that could have long-lasting consequences for the environment and humanity. Supervolcanoes like Yellowstone in the United States or the Campi Flegrei caldera in Italy are capable of ejecting massive amounts of magma and ash, covering thousands of square miles and impacting climate for years. While a supervolcano eruption is highly improbable in any given year, Baba Vanga's visions include images of large-scale volcanic events, raising the question of whether she foresaw activity from one of these powerful sites.

Baba Vanga's visions of volcanic eruptions extend to **the potential for "volcanic winters"**, where the ash and gases released into the atmosphere could lead to a temporary cooling effect on Earth's climate. Historically, such events have caused crop failures, food shortages, and economic disruptions. For instance, the eruption of Mount Tambora in 1815 resulted in the "Year Without a Summer," where unseasonably cold weather devastated agriculture across Europe and North America. Baba Vanga's prophecy for 2025 suggests that humanity could once again experience these effects, with volcanic activity challenging societies to adapt to sudden changes in climate and food availability.

Interestingly, Baba Vanga's visions of earthquakes and volcanic eruptions also hint at **symbolic meanings**, interpreted by her followers as reminders of humanity's interconnectedness with the Earth. Her followers believe that these natural disasters serve as metaphors for internal transformation and upheaval, reflecting the turbulence and shifts happening within human society. Just as tectonic plates press against each other until they release energy in sudden movements, humanity's collective struggles with social, environmental, and ethical issues may build up until they, too, reach a breaking point. In this interpretation, Baba Vanga's prophecies serve as both literal warnings and metaphors, encouraging humanity to address its internal pressures before they reach a catastrophic release.

In practical terms, Baba Vanga's predictions about earthquakes and volcanic eruptions highlight the importance of **preparedness and resilience**. Many countries prone to seismic activity have developed advanced warning systems, earthquake-resistant infrastructure, and evacuation protocols. However, if her prophecy of earthquakes in unexpected regions proves true, these areas may need to adapt rapidly, investing in emergency preparedness and educating their populations on safety measures. Her predictions remind us that disaster preparedness should be a global priority, not limited to traditionally high-risk zones.

For volcanic regions, Baba Vanga's vision underscores the need for monitoring active volcanoes and understanding their potential impacts. Scientists around the world are continuously studying volcanic activity, tracking changes in seismic activity, gas emissions, and ground deformation to predict eruptions. While predicting the exact timing and magnitude of an eruption remains challenging, advancements in monitoring technology have improved the ability to give early warnings. Baba Vanga's prophecy suggests that vigilance and scientific preparedness could make a significant difference in protecting lives and minimizing damage in the event of volcanic activity.

Her predictions also encourage a **renewed respect for nature's power**. In an era when human influence on the environment is profound, her visions remind us that Earth's forces are vast and operate on timescales far beyond human control. Earthquakes and volcanic eruptions serve as powerful reminders of this reality, showcasing the dynamic forces at work beneath our feet. Baba Vanga's prophecy suggests that humanity should approach these natural processes with humility, acknowledging that despite technological advancements, there are aspects of the Earth that remain beyond our influence.

Moreover, her prophecies of earthquakes and volcanic eruptions call for **global cooperation in disaster response and recovery**. Natural disasters often transcend national borders, as their impacts ripple across economies, supply chains, and ecosystems. In the face of such disasters, international collaboration becomes crucial for effective response, resource allocation, and recovery efforts. Baba Vanga's vision of 2025 as a year marked by geological activity encourages humanity to prioritize unity and compassion in the wake of natural crises, fostering a collective approach to resilience.

Finally, Baba Vanga's visions of earthquakes and volcanic eruptions align with her broader themes of **renewal and transformation**. While these events can be destructive, they also contribute to the Earth's renewal, shaping landscapes, forming new ecosystems, and redistributing minerals essential for life. For her followers, this cycle of destruction and rebirth holds a spiritual significance, symbolizing humanity's own journey through crisis and renewal. Her prophecy suggests that 2025 could be a year of profound change—both physically, through geological events, and spiritually, through the human response to these challenges.

As we explore Baba Vanga's predictions for 2025, her visions of earthquakes and volcanic eruptions serve as powerful reminders of the Earth's dynamic nature and humanity's place within it. Her prophecies urge us to approach these potential events with preparation, respect, and a willingness to learn from the forces that shape our world. Whether we interpret her predictions as literal forecasts or metaphors for transformation, Baba Vanga's vision offers a message of resilience, encouraging humanity to adapt, to prepare, and to find strength in the face of the Earth's immense power.

Water Crises and Floods: Baba Vanga's Warnings for 2025

Water is the essence of life, but Baba Vanga foresaw a year in which its scarcity, mismanagement, and unpredictable distribution would bring crisis to many regions of the world. In her visions for 2025, she warned of severe water-related issues, including catastrophic floods, widespread droughts, and growing water scarcity that would affect millions of people. Her predictions paint a picture of a world grappling with a "water crisis," where this vital resource becomes a source of conflict, migration, and hardship. This chapter examines her warnings about water crises and floods, exploring how they resonate with current environmental trends and what they may mean for humanity's future.

A core theme in Baba Vanga's vision is the **increasing scarcity of freshwater**. She foresaw a time when access to clean water would become one of humanity's greatest challenges, leading to social and economic strain, particularly in arid and semi-arid regions. As populations grow and climate change alters weather patterns, demand for water is rising, even as supplies dwindle. Many areas, including parts of Africa, the Middle East, and South Asia, are already experiencing significant water stress, and projections indicate that these regions could face even more severe shortages by 2025. Baba Vanga's prophecy serves as a stark reminder that water scarcity is not a distant concern but a present and worsening crisis that requires urgent attention.

One of the most troubling aspects of Baba Vanga's prophecy is her vision of **water scarcity leading to conflicts and migration**. As water resources dwindle, competition over access could exacerbate tensions between communities and even nations. She foresaw disputes arising as people struggled to secure drinking water, agricultural irrigation, and sanitation resources. Already, water disputes are simmering in regions like the Nile Basin, where multiple countries rely on the river, and the Tigris-Euphrates Basin, where tensions are high among Turkey, Syria, and Iraq. Baba Vanga's prediction of "water wars" suggests that if access to water remains unequal and unregulated, the world could see an increase in resource-based conflicts, forcing people to migrate in search of more stable access.

In addition to scarcity, Baba Vanga also predicted **extreme flooding events** in various parts of the world. Her visions included scenes of rivers overflowing, cities submerged, and entire regions forced to evacuate as water engulfed homes and infrastructure. These predictions align closely with current climate trends: as global temperatures rise, so does the intensity of rainfall, leading to more frequent and severe flooding events. Major rivers in regions such as South Asia, Southeast Asia, and Europe are particularly vulnerable to flooding, as increased rainfall combines with glacial melt and deforestation, heightening the risk of rivers spilling over into populated areas. Baba Vanga's prophecy underscores the need for resilient infrastructure and preparedness, as extreme flooding events could become a defining feature of the climate crisis in 2025.

Baba Vanga's vision of catastrophic flooding also includes **coastal inundation caused by rising sea levels**. As polar ice caps melt and thermal expansion occurs due to warming oceans, sea levels are expected to rise, posing a severe threat to coastal communities worldwide. She foresaw entire coastal areas being forced to relocate as the ocean swallowed land, forcing people to abandon their homes and livelihoods.

Low-lying regions such as Bangladesh, parts of Southeast Asia, and small island nations in the Pacific are particularly at risk. Baba Vanga's prediction warns of the potential displacement of millions of people due to coastal flooding, suggesting that 2025 could see an increase in climate refugees as communities are forced inland.

One dimension of Baba Vanga's flood predictions involves **urban areas that may be unprepared for extreme weather events**. As rainfall intensifies and storms grow more frequent, many cities with aging or inadequate infrastructure could struggle to manage the sudden influx of water. Baba Vanga foresaw scenes of overwhelmed drainage systems, waterlogged streets, and urban centers paralyzed by flooding. Cities that lack proper flood defenses or drainage infrastructure, including those in rapidly developing regions, face a higher risk of disruption. Her prophecy underscores the importance of urban planning and investment in resilient infrastructure, particularly in cities vulnerable to extreme weather. Without preparation, the social and economic costs of urban flooding could be substantial.

On the other end of the spectrum, Baba Vanga also predicted **intensified droughts and desertification**, which would exacerbate water scarcity and lead to severe agricultural disruptions. Her visions included images of parched fields, rivers running dry, and landscapes turning barren. This prophecy resonates with the reality of climate change, which has led to more prolonged and intense droughts, particularly in regions already susceptible to arid conditions. The southwestern United States, parts of Australia, sub-Saharan Africa, and regions across the Mediterranean are expected to experience increasing drought severity as temperatures rise. Baba Vanga's warning of widespread drought in 2025 serves as a reminder that water scarcity not only affects direct access to drinking water but also compromises food security and economic stability.

Baba Vanga's prophecies also hint at **mismanagement of water resources**, which could compound natural water shortages. Her followers interpret this as a critique of practices like over-extraction of groundwater, pollution of water sources, and inefficient irrigation techniques. In many parts of the world, unsustainable water usage has led to aquifer depletion, contamination of rivers and lakes, and a strain on natural ecosystems. This mismanagement has far-reaching effects, as over-extracted or polluted water sources can take decades to recover. Baba Vanga's prophecy suggests that in 2025, humanity will face the consequences of decades of mismanagement, underscoring the need for sustainable practices and conservation efforts to protect this precious resource.

In her predictions, Baba Vanga saw the water crisis not only as a physical issue but as a **moral and ethical challenge**. She believed that the crises facing humanity in 2025 would compel people to rethink their relationship with nature, particularly with essential resources like water. Her visions imply that water scarcity and floods are consequences of humanity's neglect and exploitation of the environment. For her followers, this prophecy serves as a call to action, encouraging individuals, communities, and governments to take responsibility for water stewardship, adopting sustainable practices to preserve this critical resource for future generations.

Baba Vanga's warnings about water crises also highlight the need for **global cooperation and equitable access** to water resources. As water shortages and flooding become more common, the disparities between those with access to clean water and those without will likely grow, exacerbating social and economic inequalities. She envisioned a world where water becomes a unifying concern, pushing nations to work together to ensure fair distribution and sustainable usage. Her prophecy suggests that in 2025, collaboration and international agreements on water management will be essential to avoid conflicts and support vulnerable communities.

Her prophecies on floods and water crises emphasize the importance of **disaster preparedness and community resilience**. Communities that have invested in flood defenses, efficient irrigation systems, and sustainable water management practices will be better equipped to handle these challenges. Baba Vanga's visions remind humanity of the necessity of proactive measures, from building flood barriers and rainwater harvesting systems to educating people on water conservation. These efforts, though often costly and complex, could make a significant difference in reducing the impact of water-related disasters and ensuring more stable access to water.

In exploring Baba Vanga's visions of water crises and floods, it becomes evident that her warnings are not merely forecasts of environmental turmoil but also profound lessons about humanity's connection to nature. Her prophecies challenge us to view water as a shared resource, one that requires careful stewardship and respect. She believed that addressing these challenges would require a shift in mindset—one that values sustainability, conservation, and equitable access above short-term gains.

Baba Vanga's predictions for 2025 highlight the need for immediate action in the face of the water crisis. Her warnings underscore the importance of investment in infrastructure, sustainable practices, and cooperation across borders to address both scarcity and flooding. As the effects of climate change intensify, her visions serve as a reminder that water management is not merely a local issue but a global concern, one that will shape the future of communities and nations alike.

In the chapters to follow, we will continue to explore Baba Vanga's prophecies for 2025, uncovering further insights into the environmental, social, and spiritual dimensions of her predictions. Her visions of water crises and floods call on humanity to act with urgency, compassion, and foresight, ensuring that future generations inherit a world where water remains a source of life, stability, and harmony.

Famine and Scarcity: A Global Food Crisis on the Horizon?

Among Baba Vanga's most troubling predictions for 2025 is the vision of widespread famine and food scarcity, a global crisis she foresaw impacting not only vulnerable regions but also places that have long enjoyed food security. Her prophecy paints a picture of a world struggling to feed itself, with failed crops, dwindling resources, and severe disruptions in food supply chains leading to hunger and hardship. This chapter delves into her predictions regarding famine and scarcity, examining how her warnings align with current agricultural and environmental trends, and exploring what they may signify for humanity's future.

Baba Vanga foresaw **extreme weather events** contributing to food scarcity by devastating agricultural lands and reducing crop yields. In her visions, she described "scorched earth" and "fields lying barren," a foreboding image of climate change's impact on food production. Increasingly severe droughts, floods, and storms are already affecting agriculture worldwide, and scientists predict that these extremes will only intensify as global temperatures rise. In regions where food production depends heavily on seasonal rainfall, unpredictable weather patterns can mean the difference between a plentiful harvest and complete crop failure. Baba Vanga's prophecy serves as a reminder that climate-induced disruptions could threaten the stability of food supplies in many regions.

A key factor in Baba Vanga's vision of food scarcity is **soil degradation and depletion**. She foresaw a time when soil, stripped of its nutrients and life, would become incapable of supporting crops, leading to a decline in productivity. Modern agricultural practices, such as monoculture and excessive use of chemical fertilizers and pesticides, have already contributed to soil depletion and erosion. Over time, these practices have reduced soil fertility, making it increasingly difficult to sustain large-scale agriculture. Baba Vanga's warnings suggest that without a shift toward sustainable farming methods—such as crop rotation, organic farming, and soil conservation practices—future generations could face an agricultural crisis that leaves vast tracts of land unproductive.

Baba Vanga also predicted that **water scarcity** would exacerbate the food crisis, with droughts affecting both crop irrigation and livestock farming. She described rivers running dry and water sources failing, forcing farmers to abandon their fields. In many regions, agriculture relies heavily on irrigation, but as freshwater resources become scarcer due to climate change and over-extraction, the capacity to produce food is put at risk. Water-intensive crops, like rice and wheat, could be particularly vulnerable, impacting millions who depend on these staples for sustenance. Her prophecy suggests that regions struggling with water scarcity may experience the brunt of the food crisis, pushing the world to rethink its approach to water usage and agricultural practices.

Another theme in Baba Vanga's prediction is the impact of **pest invasions and crop diseases** on food security. She foresaw plagues of insects and crop diseases spreading across regions, destroying harvests and leaving people with little to eat. As temperatures rise, pests and pathogens are able to survive in previously inhospitable climates, expanding their range and impacting new agricultural areas. For example, locust swarms in East Africa have devastated crops in recent years, and certain crop diseases have become more prevalent due to changing climate conditions.

Baba Vanga's visions remind us that climate change is not only about temperature—it can also disrupt ecological balances, creating conditions favourable for pests and diseases that harm food production.

One troubling aspect of Baba Vanga's prophecy involves the **breakdown of global food supply chains**. She foresaw disruptions in trade, with countries unable to import or export food due to political instability, economic crises, or natural disasters. In our interconnected world, food is often transported across borders, with many countries depending on imports to meet demand. However, events like pandemics, extreme weather, and trade disputes can quickly disrupt these supply chains, leading to shortages even in regions that rely on external sources for food security. Baba Vanga's vision suggests that 2025 could see greater risks to these systems, pushing countries to prioritize self-sufficiency and local food production to mitigate potential disruptions.

Baba Vanga's prophecy also hints at **rising food prices and inequality in access** to food. She envisioned a world where essential goods, especially food, would become prohibitively expensive, making it difficult for many people to afford basic sustenance. Already, rising food prices have led to increased hunger and malnutrition in vulnerable communities, and these trends are exacerbated by inflation, supply shortages, and the impact of climate change on crop yields. Her prediction serves as a warning that without addressing the root causes of rising prices and ensuring equitable access, food could become a luxury for some and a scarcity for many.

In her visions, Baba Vanga also touched on the dangers of **relying on monoculture and genetically modified crops** to sustain the world's food supply. She foresaw a time when over-reliance on a limited variety of crops would leave global agriculture vulnerable to disease and environmental change. Monoculture—the practice of growing a single crop over large areas—reduces genetic diversity, making crops more susceptible to disease outbreaks or shifts in climate. Likewise, genetically modified crops, while increasing yield, have raised concerns about their long-term effects on ecosystems and human health. Baba Vanga's warning encourages a move toward biodiversity in agriculture, promoting resilience by growing a wider variety of crops that are better suited to withstand environmental stressors.

Amid these grim warnings, Baba Vanga's prophecy also offers insights into potential solutions. She believed that humanity could overcome the food crisis by adopting sustainable, regenerative agricultural practices. Her visions included images of people returning to the land, cultivating small-scale farms, and adopting eco-friendly methods to preserve soil health and reduce dependence on synthetic chemicals. This shift toward local and sustainable food production could help alleviate the crisis by building resilience into food systems, reducing reliance on long-distance supply chains, and enhancing food security at the community level.

Baba Vanga's vision for 2025 suggests that addressing the food crisis will require not only technical solutions but also **ethical and social changes**. She believed that humanity would need to reconsider its relationship with food, treating it as a sacred resource rather than a commodity. Her prophecy calls for a reduction in food waste, a prioritization of equitable distribution, and a commitment to sustainability. For her followers, this vision is a reminder of the interconnectedness of all people and the importance of ensuring that everyone has access to the resources needed to survive and thrive.

Her predictions also highlight the importance of **international cooperation** in combating famine and food scarcity. Baba Vanga envisioned a world where nations would need to come together to share resources, knowledge, and technology to overcome these challenges. She believed that the global food crisis would push humanity toward greater collaboration, fostering a spirit of solidarity in the face of shared adversity. Her prophecy suggests that no single country can solve the food crisis alone and that addressing it will require a united, coordinated effort that transcends borders.

In examining Baba Vanga's predictions of famine and scarcity, we see a compelling call to action—a reminder that food security is a shared responsibility and a vital aspect of human well-being. Her visions challenge us to confront the vulnerabilities in our food systems, to rethink unsustainable practices, and to work toward a future where everyone has access to safe, nutritious food. They encourage a return to principles of stewardship and respect for the land, as well as a commitment to innovation and resilience.

As we continue to explore her predictions for 2025, Baba Vanga's vision of a global food crisis serves as both a cautionary tale and an opportunity. It invites us to consider how we can adapt to changing environmental conditions, reduce our impact on the planet, and ensure that food remains a source of life and health for all. Through mindful practices, cooperation, and respect for nature, humanity has the potential to avert the worst outcomes of her prophecy, building a future where food scarcity is no longer a threat but a lesson learned.

Economic Predictions for 2025: Recession or Recovery?

Baba Vanga's visions of 2025 include profound insights into the state of the global economy, a subject of critical importance as the world grapples with the challenges of inflation, debt, and economic inequality. Her predictions suggest that 2025 will be a pivotal year, marked by a crossroads between potential recession and recovery. According to her visions, the economic landscape of 2025 will be shaped by technological advancements, geopolitical tensions, and humanity's capacity for cooperation and innovation. In this chapter, we explore her economic prophecies, their alignment with current global trends, and what they might mean for the future of financial systems worldwide.

Recession on the Horizon?

Baba Vanga's warnings for 2025 include the possibility of a global recession driven by a convergence of factors. She foresaw **economic instability caused by political conflicts**, including trade wars, resource disputes, and shifting alliances. In her visions, she described a fragmented global market where cooperation breaks down, leading to economic stagnation and financial hardships for many nations. These warnings resonate with current concerns about geopolitical tensions and their impact on trade, investment, and global markets.

She also predicted that **rising debt levels and financial imbalances** could contribute to economic downturns. In recent years, many countries have faced ballooning public and private debt, driven by spending to address crises like the COVID-19 pandemic and climate adaptation. Baba Vanga's prophecy suggests that 2025 could see the consequences of unsustainable borrowing practices, with some nations struggling to service their debts, leading to defaults and ripple effects across the global financial system.

Another element of her recession warning involves **technological disruption** and its impact on traditional industries. Baba Vanga foresaw a world where automation, artificial intelligence, and digital transformation would accelerate, displacing jobs and creating significant economic shifts. While these advancements hold the potential for increased efficiency and growth, they could also lead to economic inequality if workers are not adequately supported during transitions. Her prophecy highlights the importance of addressing these disruptions to prevent long-term economic stagnation and social unrest.

Opportunities for Recovery

Despite her warnings of potential recession, Baba Vanga also saw 2025 as a year of opportunity—a time when recovery and renewal could take hold if humanity embraced collaboration and innovation. She believed that **technological advancements** could serve as a catalyst for economic growth, provided they were harnessed responsibly. Her visions included breakthroughs in clean energy, medical technologies, and digital infrastructure, which could open new markets, create jobs, and drive economic recovery.

Baba Vanga's predictions emphasized the importance of **global cooperation** in achieving economic stability. She foresaw nations coming together to address shared challenges, such as climate change and resource scarcity, creating opportunities for economic collaboration and mutual benefit. Her prophecy suggests that in 2025, international agreements on issues like carbon pricing, trade, and technological sharing could lay the groundwork for a more sustainable and equitable global economy.

Her vision also included **a rise in grassroots and local economies**, as communities adapt to global challenges by focusing on self-sufficiency and sustainability. She saw small businesses, cooperative ventures, and local production as key drivers of resilience during economic uncertainty. This prediction aligns with contemporary trends toward decentralization, where local economies gain prominence as a counterbalance to the vulnerabilities of globalized systems.

The Role of Inflation and Currency Fluctuations

Baba Vanga's economic predictions also touch on **inflation** and its destabilizing effects. She warned of rising prices for essential goods, making food, energy, and housing increasingly unaffordable for many. Her visions suggest that inflation in 2025 could be driven by supply chain disruptions, climate-related impacts on agriculture, and increased demand for limited resources. This aligns with current concerns that persistent inflation could erode purchasing power, deepen inequality, and stifle economic growth.

At the same time, she foresaw **shifts in global currencies**, with some traditional reserve currencies losing value while others gained prominence. Her prophecy hints at the possibility of alternative currencies or digital assets, such as cryptocurrencies, playing a more significant role in global finance. While digital currencies have the potential to revolutionize financial systems, they also carry risks, including volatility, regulatory challenges, and the potential for misuse. Baba Vanga's prediction underscores the importance of carefully navigating these changes to ensure stability and fairness.

Social Impacts of Economic Uncertainty

Baba Vanga's prophecy for 2025 also highlighted the **social consequences of economic challenges**. She foresaw increasing inequality, with the gap between the wealthy and the poor widening as economic instability took hold. Her visions included scenes of social unrest, protests, and demands for greater accountability from governments and corporations. This aspect of her prophecy aligns with growing concerns about economic inequality and its potential to fuel political instability and social divisions.

At the same time, she saw economic hardship driving **a renewed focus on community and shared values**. She predicted that during times of difficulty, people would come together to support one another, fostering solidarity and mutual aid. This theme of resilience through cooperation is a recurring element in her predictions, emphasizing the potential for humanity to rise above challenges through unity and collective effort.

The Environment-Economy Connection

Baba Vanga's economic predictions are closely tied to her warnings about the environment, reflecting the interconnected nature of these challenges. She foresaw the economic impacts of climate change, including costs related to disaster recovery, resource shortages, and the transition to sustainable energy. Her prophecy suggests that in 2025, addressing environmental issues will be essential to achieving economic stability, as the costs of inaction continue to mount.

She also predicted that **green technologies and sustainable industries** would become major drivers of economic growth. In her vision, investment in renewable energy, energy-efficient infrastructure, and sustainable agriculture would not only mitigate environmental damage but also create jobs and spur innovation. Her prophecy aligns with the growing recognition that a green economy could be a pathway to recovery, balancing economic development with environmental stewardship.

Lessons from Baba Vanga's Economic Prophecy

Baba Vanga's vision for 2025 offers a mix of warnings and hope, emphasizing the critical role of human choices in shaping the future of the global economy. Her prophecy challenges us to address systemic vulnerabilities, such as inequality, unsustainable practices, and reliance on debt, while also seizing opportunities for innovation and collaboration.

Key lessons from her predictions include:

- **Investing in resilience:** Strengthening financial systems, diversifying economies, and supporting local production can reduce vulnerabilities to global shocks.
- **Embracing innovation:** Advancements in technology, particularly in green energy and digital infrastructure, have the potential to drive economic recovery and long-term growth.
- **Fostering equity:** Addressing inequality through fair policies, inclusive opportunities, and global cooperation is essential to maintaining social stability and economic health.
- **Preparing for disruption:** Anticipating and mitigating the impacts of climate change, technological shifts, and geopolitical tensions will be crucial in navigating future challenges.

The Path Forward

As we approach 2025, Baba Vanga's economic predictions serve as both a warning and an inspiration. They remind us that the global economy is deeply interconnected, shaped by political, environmental, and social factors that require thoughtful and coordinated action. Her visions encourage us to face uncertainties with resilience and creativity, using the tools of innovation, cooperation, and ethical leadership to build a more stable and inclusive future.

Political Upheavals: Are Major Governments Destined to Collapse?

Baba Vanga's visions for 2025 include foreboding predictions about political upheavals, suggesting that major governments could face unprecedented challenges, instability, or even collapse. In her prophecies, she described images of power structures crumbling, alliances breaking apart, and nations struggling to maintain order amid rising social and economic tensions. These visions resonate deeply in today's politically volatile world, where shifting dynamics and global crises are testing the resilience of even the most established governments. This chapter delves into her warnings about political instability, exploring their potential causes and implications for the future.

The Collapse of Established Governments

One of the most striking aspects of Baba Vanga's prophecy is her vision of major governments struggling to maintain control in the face of internal and external pressures. She foresaw nations falling into chaos, with leadership unable to address growing divisions within their societies. Her predictions suggest that in 2025, long-standing political systems may falter under the weight of economic disparities, environmental crises, and social unrest.

In today's world, this vision aligns with the challenges many governments face: polarized electorates, diminishing public trust, and the rise of populist movements. Countries that have historically been pillars of stability are now grappling with issues like disinformation, declining institutional credibility, and deepening cultural divides. Baba Vanga's prophecy raises the question of whether these pressures could culminate in significant political shifts or even the dissolution of long-established structures.

The Role of Economic Instability

Baba Vanga's visions often connected political upheaval to economic turmoil, foreseeing a scenario where financial crises exacerbate social divisions and fuel dissatisfaction with leadership. She described scenes of protests and uprisings, with citizens demanding accountability from governments perceived as ineffective or corrupt. Economic inequality, rising inflation, and unemployment are recurring themes in her prophecies, suggesting that these factors could act as catalysts for political instability in 2025.

This prediction is particularly relevant in light of current economic trends. Many nations are grappling with the lingering effects of the COVID-19 pandemic, supply chain disruptions, and inflationary pressures, while others face mounting debt and resource shortages. If governments fail to address these issues equitably, the resulting public frustration could manifest as widespread unrest, destabilizing political systems and eroding trust in leadership.

Geopolitical Tensions and Realignments

Another theme in Baba Vanga's prophecy is the fragmentation of international alliances and the rise of new power dynamics. She foresaw a world where traditional alliances would weaken, and unexpected partnerships would emerge, reshaping the global order. This vision suggests that geopolitical tensions could reach a tipping point in 2025, leading to significant shifts in influence and power.

Her prediction aligns with current geopolitical trends, such as the rise of emerging powers like China and India, challenges to U.S. hegemony, and increasing regional rivalries. She envisioned nations struggling to adapt to a multipolar world, where cooperation becomes more challenging amid competition for resources, technological dominance, and strategic positioning. Baba Vanga's prophecy serves as a reminder of the interconnectedness of global politics and the potential for tensions in one region to ripple across the world.

The Rise of Social Movements

Baba Vanga's prophecy for 2025 includes vivid descriptions of mass protests, grassroots movements, and collective action aimed at challenging established power structures. She saw people across the globe rising against inequality, corruption, and authoritarianism, demanding greater transparency and accountability from their leaders. In her visions, these movements were both a symptom of political dysfunction and a driving force for change.

This prediction resonates with the growing prominence of social movements in recent years. From climate activism and racial justice protests to demands for democratic reforms, grassroots movements have played a pivotal role in shaping public discourse and influencing policy. Baba Vanga's vision suggests that 2025 could see an escalation of such movements, as citizens become increasingly disillusioned with traditional political systems and seek alternative pathways to justice and representation.

Authoritarianism and the Erosion of Democracy

While Baba Vanga's prophecy highlights the potential for grassroots-driven change, it also warns of the rise of authoritarianism as governments respond to instability with increased control. She foresaw leaders exploiting crises to consolidate power, curtail freedoms, and suppress dissent. This vision reflects a broader concern about the erosion of democratic norms, as some nations adopt more authoritarian measures in the name of security or stability.

Her prophecy warns that 2025 could be a critical year for the future of democracy, with nations facing stark choices about how to navigate crises. Governments that prioritize inclusivity, accountability, and resilience may emerge stronger, while those that resort to repression risk further alienating their populations and destabilizing their societies.

The Role of Technology in Political Upheaval

Baba Vanga also foresaw the growing influence of technology in shaping political dynamics, both as a tool for empowerment and as a mechanism of control. She predicted that digital technologies, including social media and artificial intelligence, would play a pivotal role in political discourse, enabling mass mobilization while also heightening polarization and disinformation.

Her prophecy highlights the dual-edged nature of technology: while it can amplify voices and connect people, it can also be weaponized to manipulate public opinion, surveil citizens, and suppress dissent. In 2025, Baba Vanga's vision suggests that the role of technology in politics will be more pronounced than ever, forcing societies to grapple with its ethical and practical implications.

Lessons from Baba Vanga's Political Prophecies

Baba Vanga's predictions of political upheaval in 2025 offer several key lessons for navigating the challenges ahead:

- **Strengthening Institutions:** Resilient political systems are essential for weathering crises. Governments must invest in transparent, accountable institutions that prioritize the needs of their citizens.
- **Addressing Inequality:** Reducing economic and social disparities can help mitigate the underlying tensions that fuel political instability.
- **Fostering Dialogue:** Open communication and collaboration between governments, citizens, and international partners are crucial for addressing shared challenges and avoiding fragmentation.
- **Balancing Security and Freedom:** Governments must find ways to maintain stability without compromising

fundamental rights and freedoms, ensuring that measures to address crises do not erode democratic principles.

- **Harnessing Technology Responsibly:** Policymakers and tech companies must work together to combat disinformation, protect privacy, and ensure that technology serves as a force for empowerment rather than oppression.

Hope Amid Uncertainty

While Baba Vanga's prophecy warns of potential political collapse, it also emphasizes the capacity for renewal and transformation. She believed that upheaval could pave the way for more inclusive, just, and resilient systems if societies rise to the challenge with courage and wisdom. Her vision suggests that 2025 could be a year of reckoning, but also of opportunity—a time to rebuild trust, strengthen governance, and prioritize the common good.

As we continue exploring her predictions, Baba Vanga's insights into political upheavals remind us of the importance of adaptability, unity, and ethical leadership. Her visions challenge us to confront the flaws in our systems and to work toward a future where power is wielded responsibly, and societies thrive in harmony with their values. In the face of uncertainty, her prophecy serves as a beacon of reflection and resilience, urging humanity to navigate the storms of change with integrity and hope.

Baba Vanga's Views on Technological Advancements in 2025

Baba Vanga's prophecies for 2025 include striking predictions about technological advancements and their profound impact on humanity. She foresaw a world transformed by breakthroughs in artificial intelligence, biotechnology, and space exploration, highlighting both the potential benefits and the risks associated with these developments. In her visions, technology played a dual role: as a tool for solving some of humanity's greatest challenges and as a force capable of creating unforeseen dilemmas. This chapter explores Baba Vanga's views on technological progress in 2025, delving into the opportunities and ethical questions her predictions raise.

The Rise of Artificial Intelligence

Baba Vanga envisioned 2025 as a year when artificial intelligence (AI) would achieve unprecedented capabilities, reshaping industries, communication, and daily life. She described machines that could think, learn, and even surpass human intelligence in certain tasks. Her prophecy aligns with current trends in AI development, where machine learning and neural networks are advancing rapidly, enabling applications in healthcare, transportation, and education.

However, Baba Vanga also warned of the dangers of unchecked AI. She foresaw scenarios where reliance on intelligent machines could lead to ethical dilemmas, including questions about privacy, autonomy, and the potential loss of jobs to automation. Her visions included images of AI systems gaining too much influence over critical decisions, challenging humanity's ability to maintain control. These warnings serve as a reminder that as AI technology evolves, it must be guided by ethical frameworks that prioritize human values and well-being.

Breakthroughs in Biotechnology

Another area Baba Vanga highlighted was biotechnology, predicting groundbreaking advancements in genetic engineering and medical science. She foresaw the development of cures for previously untreatable diseases and the ability to manipulate genetic material with precision. These visions resonate with the rise of technologies like CRISPR, which allow scientists to edit genes with remarkable accuracy, opening the door to potential treatments for genetic disorders and even the possibility of extending human life.

Despite the promise of biotechnology, Baba Vanga cautioned against its misuse. She warned that tampering with the fabric of life could have unintended consequences, including ethical debates about the boundaries of human intervention in nature. Her prophecy suggests that in 2025, humanity will face difficult questions about the use of genetic engineering, particularly in areas like human enhancement, cloning, and biosecurity. Her visions challenge society to balance innovation with responsibility, ensuring that the pursuit of progress does not come at the expense of ethics.

The Expansion of Space Exploration

Baba Vanga also foresaw significant advancements in space exploration, predicting that humanity's quest to understand the cosmos would accelerate in 2025. She envisioned breakthroughs in space travel technology, including missions to other planets and the potential discovery of extraterrestrial life. Her followers interpret these visions as a reflection of humanity's increasing focus on interplanetary exploration, driven by advancements in rocket technology and the desire to establish a human presence on Mars and beyond.

Her prophecy suggests that 2025 could be a year of monumental discoveries, possibly involving signs of life on other planets or breakthroughs in our understanding of the universe. Such milestones would not only expand scientific knowledge but also prompt philosophical and existential questions about humanity's place in the cosmos. Baba Vanga's visions encourage us to approach space exploration with curiosity and humility, recognizing its potential to unite humanity in a shared sense of wonder.

Technological Integration into Daily Life

Baba Vanga predicted that in 2025, technology would become even more integrated into daily life, blurring the lines between the physical and digital worlds. She foresaw advancements in virtual reality (VR) and augmented reality (AR), enabling immersive experiences for work, education, and entertainment. These technologies, she believed, would revolutionize how people interact with information and each other, creating new opportunities for connection and creativity.

At the same time, Baba Vanga warned of the potential for technology to isolate individuals and erode interpersonal relationships. She foresaw a world where over-reliance on digital interactions could lead to a decline in meaningful human connections. Her prophecy underscores the importance of maintaining balance, ensuring that technological tools enhance rather than replace genuine interactions and emotional bonds.

The Ethical Challenges of Technological Progress

A recurring theme in Baba Vanga's predictions is the ethical dimension of technological advancement. She believed that 2025 would be a year when humanity faced critical decisions about how to use its technological capabilities responsibly. Her visions included warnings about surveillance technologies, which could be used to monitor and control populations if left unchecked. She also cautioned against the growing divide between those who have access to advanced technologies and those who do not, emphasizing the need for equitable distribution.

Her prophecy calls for a global conversation about the ethical implications of technological progress. How can humanity ensure that advancements benefit everyone rather than a privileged few? What safeguards are needed to prevent misuse? Baba Vanga's warnings remind us that while technology has the power to transform lives, it also carries the potential for harm if not guided by clear ethical principles.

Hope and Possibility in Technological Advancements

Despite her warnings, Baba Vanga's visions of technology also carried a message of hope. She believed that if humanity harnessed its technological potential wisely, it could overcome many of its greatest challenges. Her predictions included the use of clean energy technologies to combat climate change, medical advancements to improve quality of life, and AI systems designed to enhance education and foster creativity.

She saw technology as a reflection of humanity's ingenuity and adaptability, capable of driving positive change if aligned with ethical values and a commitment to the common good. Her prophecy encourages societies to embrace innovation while remaining mindful of its consequences, ensuring that progress serves humanity as a whole.

Lessons from Baba Vanga's Technological Prophecy

Baba Vanga's predictions about technological advancements in 2025 offer several key takeaways:

- **Ethical Leadership:** The development and deployment of new technologies must be guided by ethical frameworks that prioritize human rights, equity, and sustainability.

- **Inclusive Innovation:** Ensuring access to technological advancements for all communities is essential to preventing inequality and fostering global progress.
- **Balanced Integration:** Technology should enhance human experiences without replacing the importance of real-world connections and relationships.
- **Preparedness for Change:** As technology transforms industries and societies, proactive policies and education systems are needed to help people adapt and thrive.

The Path Forward

As humanity approaches 2025, Baba Vanga's views on technological advancements serve as both a warning and an inspiration. They remind us that technology is a powerful tool, capable of shaping the future in profound ways. Her prophecies challenge us to consider not only what is possible but also what is responsible, urging us to align innovation with values that prioritize human dignity, environmental stewardship, and collective well-being.

In the chapters to come, we will continue to explore Baba Vanga's predictions, uncovering further insights into the transformative events and opportunities she envisioned for 2025. Her visions of technological progress remind us that while the future is uncertain, it is also full of potential—limited only by humanity's imagination and its commitment to using technology as a force for good.

Artificial Intelligence: Friend or Foe According to Baba Vanga?

Baba Vanga's visions of 2025 highlight the rapid rise of artificial intelligence (AI) and its transformative impact on humanity. She foresaw a world where AI would play a central role in daily life, industry, and governance, bringing immense opportunities but also profound challenges. In her prophecies, she portrayed AI as both a friend and a potential foe, emphasizing the dual-edged nature of this technology. This chapter delves into Baba Vanga's predictions about AI, exploring the balance between its promises and risks, and the ethical questions it raises.

AI as a Tool for Progress

Baba Vanga envisioned AI as a powerful tool capable of addressing some of humanity's greatest challenges. She foresaw its applications in **medicine**, where AI could revolutionize diagnostics, personalize treatments, and accelerate the development of cures for diseases. Her prophecy aligns with current advancements in AI-driven healthcare, such as algorithms that detect cancer in its early stages and predictive models that improve patient outcomes.

In addition to healthcare, Baba Vanga predicted that AI would transform **education**, making learning more accessible and personalized. She saw intelligent systems adapting to individual learning styles, helping students overcome challenges, and opening up new opportunities for lifelong education. These advancements could democratize access to knowledge, empowering people around the globe.

Baba Vanga also foresaw AI playing a critical role in **climate change mitigation and resource management**. She believed that advanced algorithms would help humanity better understand and combat environmental challenges, from optimizing renewable energy systems to predicting and preventing natural disasters. In her vision, AI served as a force for innovation, enabling solutions that were previously unimaginable.

The Risks of Unchecked AI

Despite its potential benefits, Baba Vanga warned of the dangers of unchecked AI development. She foresaw scenarios where AI systems, driven by flawed algorithms or misaligned goals, could lead to unintended consequences. One of her concerns was the potential for **job displacement**, as automation replaces human labor in industries ranging from manufacturing to finance. While AI could increase efficiency and productivity, it might also exacerbate unemployment and inequality if societies fail to adapt.

Baba Vanga also warned of the rise of **autonomous systems** that could operate beyond human control. She foresaw intelligent machines being used in warfare, describing scenarios where AI-driven weapons caused destruction without human oversight. This vision resonates with contemporary debates about the ethical implications of autonomous weapons and the need for regulations to prevent their misuse.

Another concern in her prophecy was **surveillance and loss of privacy**. Baba Vanga foresaw governments and corporations using AI to monitor citizens, raising ethical questions about data security and personal freedoms. Her vision suggests that in 2025, humanity will grapple with the balance between leveraging AI for societal benefit and protecting individual rights.

The Ethical Dilemmas of AI

A recurring theme in Baba Vanga's predictions about AI is the **ethical dimension** of its development and deployment. She believed that the technology's ultimate impact would depend on humanity's ability to guide it responsibly. Her prophecy emphasized the importance of aligning AI with values such as fairness, accountability, and transparency.

Baba Vanga's warnings also extended to the **concentration of power** in the hands of a few entities that control AI technologies. She foresaw a world where the misuse of AI could deepen inequality, creating a divide between those who benefit from the technology and those who are left behind. Her vision challenges humanity to ensure that AI serves the common good rather than perpetuating existing disparities.

AI and Human Identity

Baba Vanga's prophecy also touched on deeper philosophical questions about AI's role in shaping human identity and society. She foresaw a time when humans would become increasingly dependent on intelligent machines, raising questions about autonomy and purpose. Her vision included concerns that over-reliance on AI could erode critical thinking, creativity, and emotional connections, potentially diminishing the essence of what it means to be human.

At the same time, Baba Vanga believed that AI could inspire humanity to explore new dimensions of existence, fostering collaboration between humans and machines. She envisioned a world where AI augmented human capabilities, enabling people to reach new heights in creativity, problem-solving, and understanding.

The Potential for Harmony

Despite her warnings, Baba Vanga saw the potential for harmony between humans and AI. She believed that if guided by ethical principles, AI could become a partner in progress, enhancing humanity's ability to address challenges and unlock opportunities. Her vision included scenarios where AI systems were designed to complement human strengths, fostering a symbiotic relationship that benefited society as a whole.

Baba Vanga also emphasized the importance of education and awareness in navigating the AI revolution. She believed that equipping people with the knowledge and skills to understand and engage with AI would be essential to ensuring its responsible use. Her prophecy calls for a proactive approach, where individuals, governments, and organizations work together to shape the future of AI in a way that aligns with humanity's highest values.

Lessons from Baba Vanga's AI Prophecy

Baba Vanga's predictions about AI offer several key lessons for navigating its rapid development:

- **Ethical Leadership:** Strong ethical frameworks and regulations are essential to guiding AI's development and ensuring its alignment with human values.
- **Inclusive Innovation:** Efforts should be made to ensure that AI benefits all segments of society, reducing disparities and promoting equity.
- **Human-Centered Design:** AI systems should be designed to augment human capabilities rather than replace them, fostering collaboration and mutual benefit.
- **Transparency and Accountability:** Organizations developing AI must prioritize transparency and accountability to build trust and prevent misuse.
- **Adaptation and Education:** Preparing individuals and communities for the changes brought by AI is crucial to ensuring a smooth transition and maximizing its potential.

Hope and Responsibility

Baba Vanga's views on AI reflect a blend of hope and caution. She saw the technology as a reflection of humanity's ingenuity and adaptability, capable of transforming the world in profound ways. At the same time, she warned that its power must be guided by wisdom and responsibility, emphasizing the need for ethical leadership and collective action.

Her prophecy serves as a reminder that the future of AI is not predetermined—it is shaped by the choices humanity makes today. By approaching AI with mindfulness, collaboration, and a commitment to the greater good, society can harness its potential to create a future that aligns with the best of human aspirations.

In the chapters to come, we will continue to explore Baba Vanga's predictions, uncovering further insights into the transformative events and opportunities she envisioned for 2025. Her views on AI challenge us to navigate the complexities of technological progress with courage, integrity, and a vision for a better world.

Human Cloning and Genetic Manipulation: A 2025 Reality?

Baba Vanga's prophecies for 2025 include thought-provoking visions of advancements in biotechnology, particularly the possibilities of human cloning and genetic manipulation. These developments, while offering the potential to revolutionize medicine and human health, also raise profound ethical, social, and philosophical questions. In her visions, Baba Vanga foresaw a world grappling with the implications of reshaping life at its most fundamental level, with the promise of curing diseases and extending life counterbalanced by the risks of unintended consequences and moral dilemmas. This chapter explores her predictions about cloning and genetic manipulation, examining their alignment with current scientific progress and the challenges they pose for humanity.

The Rise of Genetic Manipulation

Baba Vanga predicted that by 2025, advances in genetic engineering would enable humanity to alter DNA with precision, allowing for the prevention of hereditary diseases, the enhancement of human capabilities, and even the creation of designer traits. Technologies like CRISPR-Cas9, which have already revolutionized gene editing, align closely with her vision. These tools allow scientists to edit genetic material with unprecedented accuracy, offering the potential to eliminate genetic disorders, improve crop resilience, and even combat climate change through engineered organisms.

Her prophecy, however, warned of the ethical dilemmas surrounding genetic manipulation. She foresaw debates about the boundaries of acceptable genetic alterations, particularly when it comes to enhancing physical or cognitive traits. Questions about equity, access, and unintended consequences loom large: Who decides which traits are desirable? Could these technologies create a genetic divide between those who can afford enhancements and those who cannot? Baba Vanga's visions challenge society to consider not just the technical possibilities of genetic manipulation but also its broader social and ethical implications.

Human Cloning: A Vision of Controversy

Baba Vanga also envisioned human cloning as a potential reality in 2025, describing scenarios where cloning could be used for medical, scientific, or even personal purposes. While cloning technologies have advanced significantly since the creation of Dolly the sheep in 1996, human cloning remains a deeply controversial topic. Baba Vanga's prophecy foresaw both the promise and the peril of cloning, highlighting its potential to save lives and advance research while also raising questions about identity, individuality, and the ethics of creating human life in a laboratory.

Her visions included the use of cloning for medical purposes, such as growing replacement organs or tissues for transplant patients. This aligns with the current field of regenerative medicine, where researchers are exploring ways to create organs from a patient's own cells, reducing the risk of rejection. Baba Vanga's prophecy suggests that in 2025, such technologies could become more widespread, offering hope to those suffering from chronic illnesses or organ failure.

However, her warnings also extended to the societal and moral consequences of cloning. She foresaw debates about the rights of cloned individuals, their status in society, and the potential misuse of cloning for unethical purposes, such as creating armies or exploiting clones for labor. Her vision challenges humanity to confront these questions before the technology becomes a reality, emphasizing the need for clear ethical guidelines and legal frameworks.

The Potential for Medical Breakthroughs

Baba Vanga's prophecy highlighted the transformative potential of genetic manipulation and cloning for medical science. She foresaw a future where these technologies could eliminate genetic disorders, extend human lifespan, and improve overall health. Her visions included breakthroughs in combating diseases like cancer, Alzheimer's, and diabetes through genetic engineering, as well as the use of cloning to generate tissues and organs tailored to individual patients.

These predictions resonate with current scientific efforts to use gene editing to treat inherited diseases and develop personalized medicine. For example, clinical trials are already exploring the use of CRISPR to treat conditions like sickle cell anemia and certain types of blindness. Baba Vanga's vision suggests that by 2025, these technologies could reach new levels of sophistication, offering hope to millions.

Ethical and Philosophical Challenges

While Baba Vanga recognized the potential benefits of cloning and genetic manipulation, she also emphasized the ethical and philosophical questions they raise. Her prophecy warned of humanity "playing God," altering the fundamental nature of life without fully understanding the consequences. She foresaw debates about the sanctity of natural processes, the potential for unintended genetic mutations, and the long-term impacts on ecosystems and human evolution.

One of the key ethical dilemmas she highlighted was the potential for creating "designer babies," where genetic traits such as intelligence, physical appearance, or athletic ability could be selected or enhanced. While this technology could eliminate certain genetic disorders, it also risks commodifying human life and reinforcing social inequalities. Baba Vanga's vision challenges society to consider where to draw the line between medical necessity and enhancement, ensuring that these technologies are used responsibly and equitably.

The Risk of Genetic Divide

Baba Vanga foresaw a world where genetic manipulation could exacerbate existing social inequalities if access to these technologies was limited to the wealthy. She described a future where genetic enhancements created a divide between those who could afford them and those who could not, leading to a new form of inequality based on genetic traits. This warning highlights the importance of ensuring that advancements in biotechnology are accessible to all, preventing the creation of a genetic underclass.

Her prophecy also warned of the potential for genetic manipulation to be used for unethical purposes, such as eugenics or the creation of genetically modified individuals for exploitation. These scenarios underscore the need for robust ethical oversight and international cooperation to prevent misuse and ensure that genetic technologies are developed in the service of humanity's collective well-being.

Balancing Progress and Responsibility

Despite her warnings, Baba Vanga believed that cloning and genetic manipulation could be forces for good if guided by ethical principles and a commitment to equity. She saw these technologies as tools for healing, innovation, and progress, capable of addressing some of humanity's most pressing challenges. Her prophecy emphasized the importance of education, awareness, and collaboration in navigating the complexities of these advancements.

Baba Vanga's vision also called for humility and respect for the natural world, reminding humanity that while technological progress is essential, it must be balanced with a deep understanding of its potential consequences. Her prophecy challenges us to approach genetic manipulation and cloning with a sense of responsibility, ensuring that these technologies serve the common good rather than individual or corporate interests.

Lessons from Baba Vanga's Prophecy

Baba Vanga's predictions about human cloning and genetic manipulation offer several key lessons for navigating this rapidly advancing field:

- **Establish Ethical Boundaries:** Clear guidelines are essential to ensure that genetic technologies are used responsibly and for the benefit of humanity.
- **Promote Equity:** Access to advancements in genetic medicine should be made equitable to prevent the creation of genetic divides.
- **Foster Global Cooperation:** International collaboration and regulation are crucial to prevent misuse and address the ethical challenges of cloning and genetic engineering.
- **Encourage Public Dialogue:** Open discussions about the implications of genetic manipulation can help societies make informed decisions about its development and use.
- **Balance Innovation with Caution:** While exploring the possibilities of genetic engineering, it is essential to consider the potential risks and long-term consequences.

The Path Forward

As humanity approaches 2025, Baba Vanga's views on cloning and genetic manipulation challenge us to navigate the opportunities and dilemmas of biotechnology with care and foresight. Her prophecy serves as both a warning and a call to action, urging societies to balance innovation with ethical responsibility and to use these advancements to build a more equitable and compassionate world.

Baba Vanga's Take on Space Exploration and Discoveries

Baba Vanga's visions of 2025 include remarkable predictions about humanity's exploration of the cosmos and ground-breaking discoveries in space science. She foresaw a time when advancements in technology and the human spirit of inquiry would push the boundaries of what is known, leading to transformative insights about the universe and our place within it. Her prophecies suggest that space exploration in 2025 will not only expand scientific understanding but also challenge humanity's philosophical and spiritual perspectives. This chapter delves into Baba Vanga's predictions on space exploration and discoveries, examining their potential implications for the future.

Accelerating Space Missions

Baba Vanga predicted that 2025 would mark a pivotal year for space exploration, with nations and private companies accelerating their efforts to explore the cosmos. She foresaw humanity making significant progress in establishing a presence beyond Earth, particularly on the Moon and Mars. Her vision included advancements in spacecraft technology, enabling longer and more efficient missions, and the development of infrastructure to support human habitation on other celestial bodies.

This prophecy aligns with current trends in space exploration. NASA, SpaceX, and other organizations are actively working toward returning humans to the Moon and launching manned missions to Mars. Projects like the Artemis program aim to establish a sustainable lunar presence as a stepping stone for deeper space exploration. Baba Vanga's vision suggests that 2025 could see key milestones in these endeavors, potentially bringing humanity closer to becoming an interplanetary species.

The Search for Extraterrestrial Life

One of Baba Vanga's most intriguing predictions is her vision of humanity discovering signs of extraterrestrial life by 2025. She described a moment of profound revelation, when evidence of life beyond Earth would reshape humanity's understanding of the universe and our place within it. Her prophecy did not specify whether this life would be microbial, intelligent, or something entirely different, leaving room for speculation.

This vision resonates with ongoing scientific efforts to search for life on other planets. Missions like NASA's Perseverance rover on Mars and the European Space Agency's JUICE mission to explore Jupiter's icy moons are designed to look for signs of past or present life. Additionally, advances in telescopes like the James Webb Space Telescope have enhanced our ability to study exoplanets and detect biosignatures in their atmospheres. Baba Vanga's prediction suggests that 2025 could bring breakthroughs in these efforts, with the potential to answer one of humanity's oldest questions: Are we alone in the universe?

Breakthroughs in Space Technology

Baba Vanga foresaw significant advancements in space technology, enabling humanity to explore the cosmos more effectively and sustainably. She envisioned spacecraft capable of traveling farther and faster, powered by innovative propulsion systems that reduce the time needed for interplanetary missions. Her prophecy suggests that new technologies, such as nuclear propulsion or advanced ion drives, could revolutionize space travel, making the dream of reaching distant planets more feasible.

In addition to propulsion, Baba Vanga predicted advancements in robotics and artificial intelligence, which would play a crucial role in space exploration. She foresaw intelligent machines conducting research in environments too hostile for humans, analyzing data, and even building infrastructure on other planets. These technologies are already in development, with robotic explorers like NASA's Mars rovers and autonomous systems for lunar construction paving the way for the future of space exploration.

Space as a Catalyst for Unity

Baba Vanga's vision of space exploration extended beyond scientific achievements to its potential as a unifying force for humanity. She believed that the shared goal of exploring the cosmos could foster collaboration among nations, transcending political and cultural differences. Her prophecy included images of international partnerships, with scientists, engineers, and astronauts from around the world working together to achieve common goals.

This vision reflects the cooperative spirit seen in initiatives like the International Space Station (ISS), where multiple countries contribute to the advancement of space science. Baba Vanga's prophecy suggests that 2025 could see an expansion of such partnerships, as humanity recognizes the importance of unity in tackling the challenges of space exploration and addressing global issues like climate change and resource scarcity.

The Philosophical Impact of Space Discoveries

Baba Vanga believed that discoveries in space would have profound philosophical and spiritual implications for humanity. She foresaw a time when understanding the vastness of the universe and the possibility of life beyond Earth would challenge traditional beliefs and inspire new ways of thinking about existence. Her prophecy included references to a "cosmic awakening," where humanity gains a deeper appreciation for the interconnectedness of all life and the mysteries of the cosmos.

This prediction aligns with the transformative effect that major scientific discoveries often have on human perspectives. The realization that Earth is not the center of the universe, or that life exists elsewhere, would undoubtedly reshape humanity's self-concept and values. Baba Vanga's vision suggests that space exploration in 2025 could be a catalyst for such shifts, encouraging a broader, more inclusive view of humanity's place in the universe.

Challenges and Ethical Considerations

While Baba Vanga was optimistic about the potential of space exploration, she also warned of challenges and ethical dilemmas. She foresaw debates about the commercialization of space, the exploitation of extraterrestrial resources, and the potential impact of human activities on other celestial bodies. Her prophecy suggests that humanity must approach space exploration with care, ensuring that it is guided by principles of sustainability and respect for the cosmos.

Baba Vanga also highlighted the risks of overreach, warning against the temptation to prioritize exploration over addressing issues on Earth. She believed that space exploration should not come at the expense of solving pressing problems such as poverty, inequality, and environmental degradation. Her vision calls for a balanced approach, where the pursuit of knowledge in space is accompanied by a commitment to improving life on our home planet.

Lessons from Baba Vanga's Space Prophecy

Baba Vanga's predictions about space exploration and discoveries offer several key lessons:

- **Foster Collaboration:** International partnerships and shared goals are essential for advancing space exploration and addressing global challenges.

- **Promote Sustainability:** Space activities must be conducted responsibly, ensuring that they do not harm the environments we explore or exacerbate inequalities on Earth.
- **Balance Exploration and Stewardship:** While expanding our horizons in space, humanity must remain committed to solving problems on Earth.
- **Embrace Wonder and Curiosity:** Space exploration offers an opportunity to inspire humanity, fostering a sense of unity and purpose in the face of the unknown.

The Path Forward

As humanity approaches 2025, Baba Vanga's vision of space exploration serves as a reminder of the limitless potential of human ingenuity and curiosity. Her prophecy challenges us to navigate the complexities of space exploration with wisdom, collaboration, and a sense of wonder, ensuring that our ventures into the cosmos benefit all of humanity.

In the chapters to come, we will continue to explore Baba Vanga's predictions, uncovering further insights into the transformative events and opportunities she envisioned for 2025. Her views on space exploration remind us that the pursuit of knowledge is not only a scientific endeavor but also a deeply human one, capable of uniting and inspiring us to reach for the stars.

Alien Contact: Did Baba Vanga Predict Interplanetary Encounters?

Among Baba Vanga's most intriguing predictions for 2025 is the possibility of alien contact—an event she foresaw as transformative for humanity. She described visions of interactions with extraterrestrial beings, suggesting that such encounters would fundamentally alter our understanding of the universe and our place within it. Baba Vanga's prophecy is both a source of fascination and debate, as it aligns with humanity's growing interest in the search for extraterrestrial life and the technological advancements enabling that quest. This chapter explores her predictions about alien contact, examining their implications and the questions they raise about the future of human civilization.

The Vision of Alien Contact

Baba Vanga envisioned a year when humanity would receive undeniable proof of extraterrestrial life. Her prophecy included imagery of communication with beings from other planets, who she described as advanced, benevolent, and eager to share knowledge with Earth. According to her visions, this contact would be initiated through signals or direct encounters, leading to breakthroughs in science, technology, and philosophy.

Her followers interpret this prediction as a reflection of humanity's readiness to engage with other intelligent civilizations. In her view, alien contact would not be random but a result of humanity reaching a level of technological and spiritual maturity that makes such interaction possible. Baba Vanga's prophecy suggests that 2025 could be a pivotal moment in the search for extraterrestrial life, bringing humanity closer to understanding its place in the cosmos.

The Search for Extraterrestrial Life

Baba Vanga's predictions align with ongoing scientific efforts to search for signs of life beyond Earth. Missions like NASA's Perseverance rover on Mars, which is analyzing soil samples for evidence of microbial life, and the European Space Agency's JUICE mission, which will study the icy moons of Jupiter, are at the forefront of this quest. Additionally, projects like the Search for Extraterrestrial Intelligence (SETI) continue to monitor the cosmos for signals from other civilizations.

Her vision also resonates with advancements in astrobiology, where scientists study extreme environments on Earth to understand where life might exist elsewhere. From deep-sea hydrothermal vents to subglacial lakes in Antarctica, these studies provide clues about the resilience of life and the potential for its existence on planets and moons within and beyond our solar system. Baba Vanga's prophecy suggests that 2025 could bring breakthroughs in these fields, possibly revealing the first evidence of extraterrestrial life.

The Nature of Alien Contact

In her visions, Baba Vanga described extraterrestrial beings as highly intelligent and technologically advanced. She believed they would come with peaceful intentions, offering humanity knowledge and guidance to address its challenges. Her prophecy included references to shared technologies that could revolutionize energy production, communication, and transportation, as well as insights into the mysteries of the universe.

However, she also warned of the potential for misunderstandings or fear, emphasizing the importance of approaching such encounters with an open mind and a spirit of cooperation. Baba Vanga's vision challenges humanity to consider how it would react to alien contact, both scientifically and culturally, and to prepare for the ethical and philosophical questions such an event would raise.

Philosophical and Spiritual Implications

Baba Vanga believed that alien contact would have profound philosophical and spiritual implications for humanity. She foresaw a time when the realization that we are not alone in the universe would challenge long-held beliefs about existence, creation, and human significance. Her prophecy suggests that such an encounter could inspire a global shift in consciousness, fostering a greater sense of unity and interconnectedness among people.

This vision aligns with the transformative impact that major discoveries in astronomy and space exploration have had throughout history. Just as the realization that Earth orbits the Sun reshaped humanity's understanding of the cosmos, the discovery of extraterrestrial life would likely lead to a reevaluation of our place in the universe. Baba Vanga's prophecy suggests that alien contact in 2025 could spark new ways of thinking about humanity's purpose and potential.

The Risks and Challenges of Alien Contact

While Baba Vanga's vision of alien contact was largely positive, she also acknowledged the risks and challenges associated with such an event. She warned of the potential for fear, mistrust, and conflict if humanity approaches extraterrestrial encounters with suspicion or hostility. Her prophecy underscores the importance of fostering a mindset of curiosity and cooperation, ensuring that any interaction is guided by mutual respect.

She also cautioned against the temptation to exploit alien knowledge or resources for selfish or destructive purposes. Baba Vanga's vision serves as a reminder that the way humanity approaches alien contact will reflect its values and priorities, shaping the outcome of such encounters for better or worse.

The Role of Technology and Science

Baba Vanga's prophecy highlighted the role of technology and science in enabling alien contact. She foresaw advancements in communication systems, telescopes, and space exploration technologies that would make it possible to detect and interact with extraterrestrial civilizations. Her vision aligns with current efforts to develop instruments capable of identifying biosignatures, technosignatures, and other evidence of alien life.

In addition to detection, she predicted the development of protocols for contact, emphasizing the need for international collaboration and ethical guidelines. Baba Vanga's prophecy suggests that 2025 could see the culmination of these efforts, with humanity better equipped to engage with intelligent life beyond Earth.

Lessons from Baba Vanga's Alien Prophecy

Baba Vanga's predictions about alien contact offer several key lessons for humanity:

- **Prepare for the Unknown:** Humanity must approach the possibility of alien contact with curiosity, humility, and an open mind.
- **Foster Global Unity:** Collaboration among nations and cultures is essential to navigating the challenges and opportunities of extraterrestrial encounters.
- **Prioritize Ethics:** Developing ethical frameworks and protocols for contact can help ensure that interactions are guided by respect and mutual benefit.
- **Embrace Change:** Alien contact would likely challenge existing beliefs and assumptions, requiring societies to adapt and evolve in response.
- **Balance Science and Spirit:** While technological advancements are crucial, alien contact also calls for

philosophical and spiritual reflection on humanity's place in the cosmos.

Hope and Responsibility

Baba Vanga's vision of alien contact is both hopeful and cautionary, emphasizing the transformative potential of such an encounter while highlighting the importance of approaching it responsibly. Her prophecy suggests that humanity stands at the threshold of a new era, where the search for life beyond Earth could lead to profound discoveries and opportunities for growth.

As we continue exploring her predictions, Baba Vanga's insights into alien contact challenge us to expand our horizons, embrace the unknown, and consider the ways in which such encounters could inspire humanity to reach its highest potential. Her vision serves as a reminder that the cosmos is vast and full of possibilities, inviting us to approach the future with wonder, curiosity, and a commitment to unity.

Social Unrest and Civil Disobedience in 2025

Baba Vanga's predictions for 2025 include vivid images of social unrest and civil disobedience, reflecting a world in turmoil as people grapple with inequality, injustice, and systemic failures. She foresaw widespread protests, uprisings, and movements demanding change, driven by dissatisfaction with political, economic, and social conditions. According to her prophecy, this unrest would stem from growing tensions between the powerful and the powerless, highlighting the urgency of addressing deep-rooted societal issues. In this chapter, we explore Baba Vanga's vision of social unrest, its potential causes, and the lessons it offers for navigating these challenges.

The Roots of Social Unrest

Baba Vanga's prophecy attributes social unrest in 2025 to a combination of factors that have been building for decades. Central to her vision is **economic inequality**, as the gap between the wealthy and the poor continues to widen. She described scenes of people rising against systems that prioritize profit over well-being, demanding fair wages, equitable access to resources, and the redistribution of wealth. These predictions resonate with contemporary concerns about income disparity, where a small percentage of the population controls the majority of wealth, leaving many struggling to meet basic needs.

Another key driver of unrest in her prophecy is **political corruption and mistrust of leadership**. Baba Vanga foresaw people losing faith in governments and institutions perceived as serving elites rather than the general population. This disillusionment, she predicted, would spark demands for transparency, accountability, and democratic reforms. Her vision reflects current global trends, where declining trust in political systems has led to protests and movements seeking systemic change.

Environmental degradation also plays a significant role in Baba Vanga's vision of unrest. She warned that the consequences of climate change—such as resource scarcity, natural disasters, and displacement—would exacerbate social tensions. As communities face the immediate impacts of environmental crises, she foresaw clashes over access to water, arable land, and safe living conditions, with marginalized groups bearing the brunt of these challenges.

The Rise of Civil Disobedience

Baba Vanga's prophecy highlights civil disobedience as a powerful tool for challenging injustice and demanding change. She envisioned a surge in nonviolent resistance, with people organizing mass protests, strikes, and boycotts to draw attention to their grievances. In her view, civil disobedience would be driven by grassroots movements, uniting individuals across cultural, political, and geographic divides.

Her vision aligns with the growing influence of social movements in recent years, from climate activism to demands for racial and gender equality. Baba Vanga predicted that in 2025, these movements would become more widespread and coordinated, leveraging digital platforms to amplify their messages and mobilize supporters. She foresaw a shift in the balance of power, as ordinary people used collective action to challenge entrenched systems and advocate for a more just and equitable world.

The Role of Technology in Social Unrest

Baba Vanga foresaw technology playing a dual role in social unrest. On one hand, she predicted that digital platforms would empower movements by facilitating communication, organization, and information sharing. Social media, livestreaming, and other technologies would enable activists to reach global audiences, bringing attention to their causes and rallying support.

On the other hand, she warned of the potential for technology to be used as a tool of surveillance and control. Governments and corporations, she foresaw, could exploit data and AI to monitor dissent, suppress protests, and manipulate public opinion. Her prophecy emphasizes the importance of safeguarding digital freedoms and ensuring that technology serves as a force for empowerment rather than oppression.

The Consequences of Unrest

Baba Vanga's visions of social unrest included both positive and negative outcomes. She foresaw moments of transformation, where collective action led to meaningful reforms, greater accountability, and the emergence of more inclusive systems. These victories, she believed, would inspire hope and demonstrate the power of unity in the face of adversity.

However, her prophecy also warned of the risks of escalation. She described scenes of violent clashes, repression, and social fragmentation, cautioning that unrest could spiral into chaos if not handled with care. Her vision challenges humanity to find constructive ways to address grievances, emphasizing dialogue, empathy, and nonviolence as essential tools for resolving conflict.

The Need for Systemic Change

Central to Baba Vanga's prophecy is the idea that social unrest is a symptom of deeper systemic issues. She believed that the root causes of inequality, corruption, and environmental degradation must be addressed to prevent further instability. Her vision called for a reevaluation of societal priorities, advocating for systems that prioritize human well-being, sustainability, and fairness over profit and power.

Her prophecy also emphasized the importance of leadership during times of unrest. She foresaw a new generation of leaders emerging from grassroots movements, bringing fresh perspectives and a commitment to ethical governance. These leaders, she believed, would play a crucial role in guiding societies through periods of upheaval and building more resilient and inclusive systems.

Lessons from Baba Vanga's Prophecy

Baba Vanga's predictions about social unrest in 2025 offer several key lessons for addressing these challenges:

- **Address Root Causes:** Tackling inequality, corruption, and environmental degradation is essential to reducing the conditions that lead to unrest.
- **Empower Grassroots Movements:** Supporting nonviolent resistance and grassroots organizing can drive meaningful change and amplify marginalized voices.
- **Safeguard Freedoms:** Protecting the rights to protest, assemble, and express dissent is crucial for fostering open and democratic societies.
- **Leverage Technology Responsibly:** Ensuring that technology is used to empower rather than suppress movements is essential for maintaining a balance of power.
- **Foster Dialogue and Reconciliation:** Encouraging open communication and empathy between conflicting

parties can help resolve tensions and build trust.

Hope Amid Turmoil

While Baba Vanga's prophecy highlights the challenges of social unrest, it also carries a message of hope. She believed that moments of upheaval could lead to growth, transformation, and the creation of more equitable systems. Her vision emphasizes the resilience of the human spirit and the potential for unity and solidarity to overcome adversity.

As humanity approaches 2025, Baba Vanga's insights into social unrest serve as a reminder of the importance of addressing systemic issues with urgency and compassion. Her prophecy challenges us to view unrest not as a threat but as an opportunity—a chance to listen, learn, and build a better future for all.

In the chapters to come, we will continue to explore Baba Vanga's predictions, uncovering further insights into the transformative events and opportunities she envisioned for 2025. Her vision of social unrest reminds us that even in the face of turmoil, there is the potential for progress and renewal, driven by the collective power of humanity to demand and create change.

Youth Movements and the Rise of a New World Order

Baba Vanga's predictions for 2025 include a compelling vision of youth-led movements reshaping the global landscape, ushering in what she described as a "new world order." According to her prophecy, the younger generation would emerge as a driving force for change, challenging outdated systems, advocating for justice, and addressing urgent global issues. This chapter explores her vision of youth movements, their potential influence, and the transformative role they could play in creating a more equitable and sustainable world.

The Rise of Youth Activism

Baba Vanga foresaw a surge in youth activism, with young people mobilizing around issues such as climate change, social justice, and political reform. She described scenes of young leaders rallying their peers, using digital platforms to amplify their voices and organize large-scale movements. Her prophecy highlights the energy, creativity, and resilience of the younger generation, suggesting that their efforts would be pivotal in shaping the future.

This vision aligns with current trends, where youth-led movements like Fridays for Future, Extinction Rebellion, and global protests for racial and gender equality have demonstrated the power of young people to drive change. Baba Vanga's prediction suggests that in 2025, these movements will gain even greater momentum, with young activists taking on leadership roles and influencing policy at local, national, and international levels.

Challenging the Status Quo

Baba Vanga believed that youth movements would challenge entrenched systems of power and inequality, demanding accountability from governments, corporations, and institutions. She foresaw young people rejecting outdated practices and ideologies, advocating for progressive policies that prioritize human rights, environmental sustainability, and social equity.

Her vision included bold actions, such as mass protests, boycotts, and grassroots campaigns aimed at disrupting systems that perpetuate harm. Baba Vanga's prophecy suggests that in 2025, youth movements will not only highlight the flaws in existing systems but also propose innovative solutions, leveraging their unique perspectives and skills to drive meaningful change.

The Role of Technology

Baba Vanga foresaw technology playing a central role in empowering youth movements. She envisioned young people using digital platforms to connect, collaborate, and share ideas across borders, creating a global network of activists united by common goals. Her prophecy highlights the potential of social media, online petitions, and virtual organizing tools to amplify the voices of young people and bring attention to their causes.

At the same time, Baba Vanga warned of the risks associated with technology, including misinformation, surveillance, and the potential for digital activism to become performative rather than impactful. Her vision challenges youth movements to navigate these challenges thoughtfully, ensuring that their use of technology enhances their efforts and fosters genuine change.

Creating a New World Order

Baba Vanga's prophecy included the rise of what she called a "new world order," led by the principles and values championed by youth movements. She envisioned a global shift toward systems that prioritize cooperation, equity, and sustainability, replacing structures rooted in greed and exploitation. According to her vision, this transformation would be driven by young people who refuse to accept the status quo and who work tirelessly to build a better future.

This new world order, as Baba Vanga described it, would emphasize global solidarity, with nations collaborating to address shared challenges such as climate change, poverty, and inequality. She foresaw young leaders taking on roles in politics, business, and community organizing, bringing fresh perspectives and innovative approaches to these issues.

The Challenges of Leadership

While Baba Vanga's prophecy highlighted the potential of youth movements to create change, she also acknowledged the challenges they would face. She warned of resistance from established powers, who may view these movements as a threat to their authority. Her vision included scenes of young activists navigating obstacles such as censorship, repression, and co-optation, emphasizing the importance of resilience and unity in overcoming these challenges.

Baba Vanga also foresaw the risks of internal divisions within youth movements, cautioning that disagreements over strategies and priorities could undermine their effectiveness. Her prophecy suggests that collaboration, communication, and a shared commitment to their goals will be essential for the success of these movements.

The Impact on Global Governance

Baba Vanga believed that youth movements would have a profound impact on global governance, inspiring reforms that make institutions more inclusive, transparent, and accountable. She foresaw young people advocating for policies that address systemic inequalities, protect the environment, and promote peace and human rights. Her vision suggests that by 2025, these efforts could lead to significant changes in how power is distributed and exercised on a global scale.

Her prophecy also emphasized the importance of education and empowerment in supporting youth leadership. She believed that providing young people with the tools, knowledge, and opportunities to succeed would be critical to ensuring their ability to drive change and shape the future.

Lessons from Baba Vanga's Prophecy

Baba Vanga's predictions about youth movements and the rise of a new world order offer several key lessons for navigating this transformative period:

- **Support Youth Leadership:** Empowering young people through education, mentorship, and resources can help them realize their potential as change-makers.
- **Foster Collaboration:** Building bridges between generations, cultures, and movements can strengthen efforts to address shared challenges.
- **Champion Inclusivity:** Ensuring that youth movements are diverse and representative can enhance their legitimacy and effectiveness.
- **Navigate Challenges Thoughtfully:** Preparing for obstacles such as resistance and division can help movements remain resilient and focused on their goals.
- **Embrace Innovation:** Leveraging technology and creativity can amplify the impact of youth-led initiatives and inspire new solutions to complex problems.

Hope for the Future

Baba Vanga's vision of youth movements and a new world order is ultimately one of hope. She believed that the passion, ingenuity, and determination of young people could overcome even the most daunting challenges, creating a world that is more just, equitable, and sustainable. Her prophecy serves as a reminder that while the path to change may be difficult, it is also filled with possibility.

As humanity approaches 2025, Baba Vanga's insights challenge us to recognize and support the transformative potential of youth movements. Her vision inspires us to embrace the energy and vision of the younger generation, working together to build a future that reflects the best of humanity's values and aspirations.

In the chapters to come, we will continue to explore Baba Vanga's predictions, uncovering further insights into the transformative events and opportunities she envisioned for 2025. Her views on youth movements remind us that the future is shaped by those who dare to dream and act, and that the power to create a better world lies within us all.

The Spiritual Awakening of Humanity in 2025

Baba Vanga's visions for 2025 include a profound spiritual awakening for humanity—a time when people collectively seek deeper meaning, connection, and purpose in the face of global challenges. She foresaw a shift in consciousness, where individuals and societies move beyond material concerns and embrace values rooted in compassion, unity, and understanding. This awakening, she believed, would transform the way humanity approaches life, relationships, and the natural world, setting the stage for a more harmonious future. In this chapter, we explore Baba Vanga's prediction of spiritual awakening, its potential catalysts, and its implications for humanity.

The Catalysts for Awakening

Baba Vanga's prophecy suggests that the spiritual awakening of 2025 would be driven by a convergence of crises and breakthroughs. She foresaw humanity confronting existential challenges—such as climate change, social unrest, and economic inequality—that force people to reevaluate their priorities and seek deeper meaning. At the same time, she predicted advancements in science and technology, particularly in space exploration and AI, that would expand humanity's understanding of existence and inspire awe and wonder.

Her vision also included a growing recognition of humanity's interconnectedness, both with each other and with the natural world. She believed that as people face shared challenges, they would begin to see themselves as part of a larger whole, fostering empathy, cooperation, and a sense of collective responsibility. This shift in perspective, she predicted, would be a key driver of spiritual awakening.

The Role of Crises in Transformation

Baba Vanga often emphasized the transformative power of crises, viewing them as opportunities for growth and renewal. In her prophecy for 2025, she described a world grappling with upheaval but also on the verge of profound transformation. She believed that adversity could inspire individuals and societies to reflect on their values, let go of outdated beliefs, and embrace new ways of thinking and being.

This vision aligns with historical patterns, where periods of turmoil have often sparked spiritual and philosophical movements. Baba Vanga's prophecy suggests that the challenges of 2025 could similarly act as a catalyst for awakening, prompting humanity to seek meaning and purpose beyond material pursuits.

The Emergence of Global Unity

A central theme in Baba Vanga's vision of spiritual awakening is the emergence of a sense of global unity. She foresaw people transcending cultural, religious, and national boundaries to embrace a shared identity as members of the human family. This shift, she believed, would be driven by the realization that humanity's survival depends on cooperation and mutual respect.

Her prophecy included images of diverse communities coming together to address common challenges, from environmental conservation to social justice. She believed that this unity would be rooted in a shared recognition of the sacredness of life and the interconnectedness of all beings. Baba Vanga's vision challenges humanity to move beyond divisions and embrace a collective sense of purpose and responsibility.

A Return to Spiritual Practices

Baba Vanga predicted a resurgence of interest in spiritual practices as people seek guidance and grounding during times of uncertainty. She foresaw a revival of meditation, mindfulness, and other contemplative traditions that help individuals connect with their inner selves and cultivate a sense of peace and clarity.

She also envisioned people turning to ancient wisdom and indigenous knowledge for insights into living in harmony with nature and each other. Her prophecy suggests that these practices and teachings could play a vital role in fostering the spiritual awakening of 2025, offering tools for navigating the challenges and opportunities of the time.

The Role of Technology in Spiritual Growth

While Baba Vanga often warned of the potential dangers of technology, she also recognized its potential to support spiritual awakening. She foresaw advancements in virtual reality, artificial intelligence, and neuroscience that could help people explore consciousness, connect with others, and access transformative experiences.

Her vision included the use of technology to spread messages of hope, wisdom, and compassion, creating a global network of support and inspiration. At the same time, she cautioned against becoming overly reliant on technology, emphasizing the importance of maintaining a balance between digital tools and direct, personal experiences.

The Transformation of Values

Baba Vanga believed that the spiritual awakening of 2025 would lead to a fundamental transformation of societal values. She foresaw a shift away from materialism and individualism toward a focus on community, sustainability, and spiritual fulfillment. In her vision, people would prioritize relationships, purpose, and well-being over wealth and status, creating a more compassionate and equitable world.

This transformation, she predicted, would also extend to institutions and systems, with governments, businesses, and organizations embracing ethical and sustainable practices. Baba Vanga's prophecy challenges humanity to align its values and actions with principles that support the common good and the health of the planet.

Challenges on the Path to Awakening

While Baba Vanga's prophecy of spiritual awakening is hopeful, she also acknowledged the challenges involved in such a transformation. She foresaw resistance from those who cling to old ways of thinking and acting, as well as the potential for conflicts over differing visions of the future. Her vision emphasizes the importance of patience, dialogue, and empathy in navigating these challenges.

She also warned of the temptation to seek quick fixes or superficial solutions, cautioning that true awakening requires deep reflection and commitment. Baba Vanga's prophecy suggests that the journey to spiritual awakening is both individual and collective, requiring effort and intention from all members of society.

Lessons from Baba Vanga's Spiritual Prophecy

Baba Vanga's predictions about the spiritual awakening of 2025 offer several key lessons for fostering this transformation:

- **Embrace Reflection:** Times of crisis can be opportunities for growth if approached with a willingness to reflect and learn.

- **Foster Connection:** Building relationships and cultivating empathy are essential for creating a sense of global unity.
- **Practice Mindfulness:** Engaging in spiritual practices can help individuals navigate uncertainty and find meaning and purpose.
- **Promote Ethical Values:** Aligning actions with principles of compassion, sustainability, and justice supports the collective awakening.
- **Balance Technology and Humanity:** Leveraging technology for spiritual growth while maintaining personal connections ensures a holistic approach.

Hope for a Harmonious Future

Baba Vanga's vision of spiritual awakening is ultimately one of hope, offering a glimpse of a future where humanity moves beyond division and conflict to embrace unity and purpose. She believed that the challenges of 2025, while daunting, would inspire a collective shift toward values that honor the interconnectedness of all life.

As we continue to explore her predictions, Baba Vanga's insights challenge us to approach the future with openness, compassion, and a commitment to growth. Her vision reminds us that even in the face of uncertainty, the potential for transformation and renewal is always within reach, guided by the enduring power of the human spirit.

The Role of Religion and Spirituality in the New World

Baba Vanga's visions for 2025 include a significant evolution in the roles of religion and spirituality within a rapidly transforming world. She foresaw a time when traditional religious institutions would face challenges, yet spirituality would flourish as individuals seek deeper meaning and connection. Her prophecy suggested that humanity would embrace a more inclusive and universal approach to faith, emphasizing shared values over doctrinal differences. This chapter explores Baba Vanga's predictions about the shifting roles of religion and spirituality, and their implications for the new world she envisioned.

The Transformation of Organized Religion

Baba Vanga predicted that 2025 would mark a turning point for organized religions. She foresaw declining influence for institutions that fail to adapt to the changing needs and values of their followers. In her visions, she described a growing disillusionment with dogma and hierarchy, as people seek faith experiences that feel more personal, inclusive, and relevant to contemporary life.

This prophecy aligns with current trends in which traditional religious attendance is declining in many parts of the world, particularly among younger generations. Baba Vanga's vision suggests that religious institutions will face pressure to evolve, adopting practices and teachings that resonate with a more spiritually aware and globally connected humanity.

The Rise of Spirituality

While organized religion may face challenges, Baba Vanga foresaw a flourishing of spirituality, with individuals exploring diverse practices and philosophies to deepen their understanding of existence. She believed that spirituality in 2025 would move beyond traditional frameworks, encompassing meditation, mindfulness, and holistic approaches that emphasize inner growth and universal connection.

Her vision also included a blending of spiritual traditions, as people draw wisdom from multiple sources to create personalized paths to meaning. This inclusivity, she predicted, would foster greater understanding and harmony among people of different backgrounds, reducing conflicts based on religious differences.

Religion as a Unifying Force

Baba Vanga believed that despite the challenges faced by traditional religions, their core teachings could serve as a unifying force in the new world. She foresaw a shift in focus from doctrines and rituals to the shared values that underlie all faiths, such as compassion, love, and the pursuit of truth.

In her vision, interfaith dialogue and collaboration would play a key role in addressing global challenges, from poverty to climate change. She believed that religious and spiritual leaders would work together to inspire collective action, emphasizing humanity's shared responsibility to care for one another and the planet.

The Role of Technology in Spiritual Evolution

Baba Vanga also foresaw technology influencing the way people engage with religion and spirituality. She envisioned digital platforms enabling global access to spiritual teachings, connecting seekers with mentors, and creating virtual communities for worship and reflection. This democratization of spiritual knowledge, she believed, would empower individuals to explore faith on their own terms.

At the same time, she cautioned against the over-commercialization of spirituality, warning that technology could be used to exploit rather than enlighten. Baba Vanga's prophecy emphasizes the importance of maintaining authenticity and integrity in the integration of technology with spiritual practices.

The Search for Universal Truths

Baba Vanga's prophecy included a deepening interest in universal truths that transcend individual religions. She foresaw a growing recognition of the interconnectedness of all life and the spiritual principles that unite humanity. This shift, she predicted, would inspire a global movement toward unity and cooperation, as people focus on their shared humanity rather than their differences.

Her vision challenges individuals and societies to move beyond rigid boundaries, embracing an inclusive approach to spirituality that honors diverse perspectives while seeking common ground. Baba Vanga believed that this pursuit of universal truths would play a central role in shaping the values and priorities of the new world.

The Role of Spiritual Leaders

Baba Vanga foresaw a new generation of spiritual leaders emerging in 2025, individuals who inspire through their actions rather than their titles. These leaders, she predicted, would prioritize service, humility, and the empowerment of others, guiding humanity through times of uncertainty and transformation.

Her vision included both established religious figures who adapt to the needs of the time and grassroots leaders who emerge from communities to address local challenges. Baba Vanga believed that these leaders would play a crucial role in fostering hope, resilience, and collective purpose during periods of upheaval.

Challenges to Overcome

While Baba Vanga's prophecy is hopeful, she also acknowledged the challenges involved in redefining the roles of religion and spirituality. She foresaw resistance from institutions and individuals who cling to traditional structures, as well as the potential for division and conflict during periods of change.

Her vision also highlighted the risks of superficial engagement with spirituality, where people seek quick fixes or trends rather than meaningful growth. Baba Vanga's prophecy challenges humanity to approach these transformations with sincerity, openness, and a commitment to authenticity.

Lessons from Baba Vanga's Prophecy

Baba Vanga's predictions about religion and spirituality in the new world offer several key lessons for navigating this evolution:

- **Embrace Inclusivity:** Recognizing the shared values and principles across faiths can foster unity and understanding.
- **Focus on Service:** Spirituality and religion should prioritize actions that benefit individuals, communities, and the planet.
- **Leverage Technology Wisely:** Using digital tools to share knowledge and connect people can enhance spiritual growth if approached with integrity.
- **Seek Universal Truths:** Exploring common principles that transcend individual beliefs can inspire collective purpose and cooperation.

- **Support Authentic Leaders:** Elevating leaders who embody compassion and wisdom can guide humanity through periods of transformation.

Hope for a Spiritual Renaissance

Baba Vanga's vision of religion and spirituality in 2025 is ultimately one of renewal and growth. She believed that the challenges faced by traditional institutions would pave the way for a more inclusive and compassionate approach to faith, inspiring humanity to connect with deeper truths and shared values. Her prophecy suggests that this spiritual renaissance could play a vital role in addressing global challenges and creating a more harmonious world.

As we continue to explore her predictions, Baba Vanga's insights challenge us to embrace the transformative power of spirituality, honoring its potential to unite and uplift humanity. Her vision reminds us that in the face of uncertainty, the search for meaning and connection can illuminate the path forward, offering hope and purpose in the journey toward a better future.

Baba Vanga on Health Pandemics and Medical Advancements

Baba Vanga's predictions for 2025 include insights into the state of global health, warning of potential pandemics while also envisioning groundbreaking medical advancements. She foresaw a world grappling with challenges to public health, including the spread of infectious diseases and the strain on healthcare systems. At the same time, her prophecy highlighted humanity's capacity for innovation, predicting transformative breakthroughs in medicine and technology that could revolutionize healthcare. This chapter explores Baba Vanga's views on health pandemics and medical advancements, examining their potential impact on humanity.

The Threat of New Pandemics

Baba Vanga warned that 2025 could see the emergence of new pandemics, driven by factors such as climate change, globalization, and urbanization. She foresaw pathogens spreading rapidly due to changing environmental conditions, increased human-wildlife interaction, and global interconnectedness. Her prophecy described scenes of overwhelmed healthcare systems and communities struggling to contain outbreaks.

This warning aligns with contemporary scientific concerns about zoonotic diseases—those that jump from animals to humans—becoming more prevalent as ecosystems are disrupted. Baba Vanga's vision suggests that humanity must remain vigilant, investing in early detection systems, public health infrastructure, and global collaboration to prevent and respond to pandemics.

Lessons from Recent Pandemics

Baba Vanga's prophecy also emphasized the importance of learning from past pandemics to prepare for future challenges. She believed that the lessons of the COVID-19 pandemic—such as the need for rapid vaccine development, equitable access to healthcare, and coordinated international responses—would shape humanity's ability to navigate future crises.

Her vision included the development of advanced surveillance systems that use artificial intelligence and big data to identify potential outbreaks before they spread. She foresaw nations working together to share information and resources, recognizing that public health is a global responsibility.

Breakthroughs in Medicine and Biotechnology

While Baba Vanga warned of health challenges, she also predicted remarkable advancements in medicine and biotechnology that would transform healthcare by 2025. She foresaw breakthroughs in genetic engineering, personalized medicine, and regenerative therapies, enabling doctors to treat diseases with unprecedented precision and effectiveness.

One of her most hopeful predictions was the development of cures for conditions previously considered incurable. Her prophecy included advancements in gene editing technologies, such as CRISPR, allowing scientists to correct genetic defects and prevent hereditary diseases. She also envisioned the widespread use of stem cell therapies to repair damaged tissues and organs, offering new hope to patients with chronic illnesses or injuries.

The Role of Artificial Intelligence in Healthcare

Baba Vanga believed that artificial intelligence (AI) would play a central role in advancing medical science. She foresaw AI-driven systems revolutionizing diagnostics, enabling early detection of diseases through advanced imaging and data analysis. In her vision, AI would also enhance drug discovery, reducing the time and cost required to develop new treatments.

Her prophecy highlighted the potential of AI to improve healthcare accessibility, particularly in underserved regions. She envisioned intelligent systems providing remote consultations, monitoring patients, and delivering personalized care plans. Baba Vanga's vision suggests that AI could help bridge gaps in healthcare equity, ensuring that more people benefit from medical advancements.

Vaccines and Global Immunization

Baba Vanga foresaw significant progress in vaccine development, predicting that by 2025, scientists would create more effective and universal vaccines. Her prophecy included the development of vaccines capable of targeting multiple strains of a pathogen, reducing the need for frequent updates and increasing long-term efficacy.

She also envisioned global immunization campaigns becoming more efficient and widespread, driven by advancements in vaccine storage, distribution, and administration. Her vision emphasized the importance of equitable access to vaccines, ensuring that even the most vulnerable populations are protected from infectious diseases.

Mental Health and Holistic Approaches

In addition to physical health, Baba Vanga's prophecy highlighted the growing importance of mental health in 2025. She foresaw increased recognition of the psychological impacts of pandemics, social isolation, and modern stressors, prompting a shift toward more holistic approaches to healthcare.

Her vision included advancements in mental health treatments, such as neurotechnologies that address conditions like depression and anxiety, as well as the integration of mindfulness and alternative therapies into mainstream care. Baba Vanga believed that addressing mental and emotional well-being would be essential for building resilience and fostering overall health.

The Ethical Challenges of Medical Advancements

While Baba Vanga was optimistic about medical progress, she also warned of the ethical dilemmas that could arise. She foresaw debates over the use of genetic engineering, AI, and other technologies, emphasizing the need for clear guidelines to ensure these advancements are used responsibly.

Her prophecy also highlighted concerns about healthcare equity, cautioning that the benefits of medical breakthroughs must be accessible to all, not just the privileged few. Baba Vanga believed that addressing these ethical challenges would be critical to ensuring that medical advancements serve humanity's collective well-being.

The Role of Collaboration and Innovation

Baba Vanga's vision emphasized the importance of global collaboration and innovation in addressing health challenges. She believed that by working together, nations could pool their resources and expertise to develop solutions that benefit everyone. Her prophecy included images of scientists, healthcare workers, and policymakers uniting to tackle pandemics, improve healthcare systems, and advance medical science.

Her vision also encouraged individuals to take an active role in their health, promoting preventative care, healthy lifestyles, and a proactive approach to well-being. Baba Vanga believed that empowering people to make informed decisions about their health would be key to building a healthier world.

Lessons from Baba Vanga's Prophecy

Baba Vanga's predictions about health pandemics and medical advancements offer several key lessons:

- **Invest in Prevention:** Strengthening public health systems and investing in early detection can help prevent and contain pandemics.
- **Promote Equity:** Ensuring access to healthcare and medical advancements for all populations is essential for global well-being.
- **Embrace Innovation:** Leveraging technologies like AI and genetic engineering can drive transformative progress in medicine.
- **Address Mental Health:** Integrating mental and emotional well-being into healthcare is critical for fostering resilience and overall health.
- **Navigate Ethical Challenges:** Establishing clear guidelines and prioritizing ethics can help ensure that medical advancements benefit humanity responsibly.

Hope for a Healthier Future

Baba Vanga's vision of health in 2025 is one of both caution and hope. While she warned of the potential for pandemics and health crises, she also believed in humanity's capacity for innovation, collaboration, and resilience. Her prophecy challenges us to approach health with a holistic perspective, recognizing the interconnectedness of physical, mental, and social well-being.

As we continue to explore her predictions, Baba Vanga's insights inspire us to strive for a future where healthcare is accessible, advancements are guided by ethics, and humanity works together to build a healthier and more equitable world. Her vision reminds us that even in the face of challenges, the pursuit of knowledge and compassion can illuminate the path to healing and progress.

Disease Outbreaks and the Potential for a Global Pandemic

Baba Vanga's predictions for 2025 included a stark warning about the potential for disease outbreaks and a global pandemic. Her visions described a world where humanity faces challenges in controlling the spread of new pathogens, compounded by environmental changes, globalization, and evolving human behavior. While her prophecy underscored the risks of widespread illness, it also highlighted humanity's capacity for resilience, innovation, and collaboration in mitigating such crises. This chapter explores her predictions about disease outbreaks and the lessons they offer for preparing for and responding to future pandemics.

The Warning Signs of a Global Pandemic

Baba Vanga foresaw the emergence of new pathogens in 2025, driven by factors such as climate change, deforestation, and increased human-wildlife interaction. She described these pathogens as potentially more contagious and harder to control due to mutations and resistance to existing treatments. Her visions included images of healthcare systems under strain, communities in quarantine, and a race against time to develop effective countermeasures.

Her prophecy resonates with contemporary concerns in epidemiology, where scientists warn of the "spillover effect," where diseases jump from animals to humans. Deforestation, urbanization, and wildlife exploitation disrupt ecosystems, increasing the likelihood of contact between humans and disease-carrying species. Baba Vanga's vision serves as a reminder that addressing these root causes is essential to preventing future pandemics.

The Role of Climate Change

A central theme in Baba Vanga's prophecy is the role of climate change in exacerbating disease outbreaks. She foresaw rising temperatures, shifting weather patterns, and melting permafrost releasing ancient pathogens that had been dormant for centuries. Her vision included an increase in vector-borne diseases, such as malaria and dengue fever, as warming climates expand the habitats of mosquitoes and other carriers.

This aspect of her prophecy aligns with scientific findings that climate change is already impacting the spread of diseases. Baba Vanga's warning underscores the need for a holistic approach to pandemic prevention, one that addresses environmental sustainability alongside public health measures.

Globalization and Rapid Spread

Baba Vanga predicted that the interconnectedness of the modern world would accelerate the spread of diseases, making containment more challenging. She foresaw outbreaks traveling across borders through international trade, travel, and migration, with densely populated urban areas becoming hotspots for transmission.

Her prophecy highlights the importance of global cooperation in responding to pandemics. She envisioned nations sharing information, resources, and expertise to control outbreaks and mitigate their impact. Baba Vanga's vision suggests that in 2025, humanity must embrace a collective approach to pandemic preparedness, recognizing that diseases do not respect borders.

The Importance of Early Detection and Preparedness

A key lesson from Baba Vanga's prophecy is the importance of early detection systems and preparedness. She foresaw advancements in surveillance technologies, including artificial intelligence and genomic sequencing, enabling scientists to identify and track new pathogens quickly. Her vision also emphasized the role of public health infrastructure, including testing, contact tracing, and vaccination campaigns, in preventing outbreaks from escalating.

Baba Vanga's prediction aligns with current efforts to improve global health security. Initiatives such as the World Health Organization's (WHO) Global Outbreak Alert and Response Network (GOARN) aim to strengthen the ability of nations to detect and respond to emerging diseases. Her prophecy suggests that by 2025, such systems could become even more critical in safeguarding public health.

The Race for Vaccines and Treatments

In her prophecy, Baba Vanga foresaw a rapid acceleration in the development of vaccines and treatments during disease outbreaks. She described breakthroughs in biotechnology, including universal vaccines capable of targeting multiple strains of a virus, reducing the need for frequent updates. Her vision also included advancements in antiviral drugs and monoclonal antibodies, providing effective tools to combat new pathogens.

Baba Vanga's prediction suggests that 2025 could see the culmination of these efforts, with medical science achieving new milestones in pandemic response. Her vision emphasizes the importance of investing in research and development, ensuring that humanity is equipped to address emerging health threats.

Equity and Accessibility

While Baba Vanga's prophecy highlighted scientific advancements, she also warned of the risks of inequitable access to healthcare. She foresaw disparities in the availability of vaccines, treatments, and resources, with vulnerable populations bearing the brunt of disease outbreaks. Her vision called for a commitment to global health equity, ensuring that no one is left behind in the fight against pandemics.

Her prophecy challenges policymakers, healthcare organizations, and pharmaceutical companies to prioritize affordability and accessibility in the development and distribution of medical interventions. Baba Vanga believed that addressing these disparities is essential for achieving effective and inclusive pandemic response.

The Social and Economic Impact of Pandemics

Baba Vanga's visions of a global pandemic also included its far-reaching social and economic consequences. She foresaw disruptions to supply chains, labor markets, and education systems, as well as the psychological toll of isolation and uncertainty. Her prophecy emphasized the importance of resilience, both at the individual and societal levels, in navigating these challenges.

Her vision also included the potential for positive change, as pandemics force societies to reevaluate their priorities and invest in systems that promote well-being and sustainability. Baba Vanga's prophecy suggests that while pandemics can be devastating, they also present opportunities for growth and transformation.

Lessons from Baba Vanga's Prophecy

Baba Vanga's predictions about disease outbreaks and global pandemics offer several key lessons:

- **Address Root Causes:** Preventing pandemics requires addressing environmental and social factors that contribute to the emergence of new diseases.
- **Invest in Preparedness:** Strengthening public health infrastructure and early detection systems is critical for

effective pandemic response.

- **Foster Global Cooperation:** Collaborative efforts are essential to controlling outbreaks and ensuring equitable access to resources.
- **Accelerate Innovation:** Advancements in vaccines, treatments, and diagnostics can save lives and mitigate the impact of pandemics.
- **Promote Resilience:** Building systems that support mental health, economic stability, and community solidarity can help societies recover and thrive.

Hope amid Challenges

Baba Vanga's vision of pandemics is both a warning and a call to action. While she foresaw the potential for devastating outbreaks, she also believed in humanity's capacity to rise to the challenge through innovation, collaboration, and compassion. Her prophecy reminds us that the fight against pandemics is not just a medical or scientific endeavor—it is a collective effort that requires the participation and commitment of individuals, communities, and nations.

As we continue to explore her predictions, Baba Vanga's insights inspire us to take proactive steps to safeguard public health and build a future where humanity is better prepared to face the uncertainties ahead. Her vision challenges us to approach health crises with resilience and determination, transforming adversity into an opportunity for growth and progress.

Global Power Shifts: East Meets West in Baba Vanga's Prophecies

Baba Vanga's visions for 2025 include a dynamic shift in global power, with Eastern nations gaining influence and reshaping the international balance of power. She foresaw a world where East and West converge, blending perspectives, resources, and strengths to address global challenges. According to her prophecy, this shift would not only transform geopolitical dynamics but also foster a new era of cultural and intellectual exchange, as humanity learns to embrace diverse ways of thinking and problem-solving. In this chapter, we explore Baba Vanga's predictions about the global power shift, the implications of East and West collaboration, and the challenges and opportunities this transition might bring.

The Rise of the East

Baba Vanga predicted that Eastern nations, particularly China and India, would emerge as key players on the global stage by 2025. She foresaw their economic, technological, and political influence expanding, challenging the traditional dominance of Western powers. Her prophecy included images of Eastern nations leading advancements in technology, energy, and trade, positioning themselves at the forefront of global progress.

This vision aligns with contemporary trends, as Asia's rapid economic growth and technological innovation continue to reshape global markets. China's Belt and Road Initiative, for instance, represents a significant step toward creating a globally connected infrastructure network. Baba Vanga's prediction suggests that Eastern influence will only continue to grow, reshaping economic and political relationships worldwide.

The Decline of Western Dominance

While Baba Vanga did not predict the fall of Western nations, she foresaw a decline in their unilateral control over global affairs. She believed that Western powers would continue to play significant roles but would need to adapt to a more multipolar world where power is more evenly distributed. This shift, she predicted, would require Western nations to prioritize diplomacy, cooperation, and mutual respect, recognizing the benefits of balanced global partnerships.

Her vision resonates with recent geopolitical developments, where Western nations are increasingly navigating complex relationships with emerging Eastern powers. Baba Vanga's prophecy suggests that by 2025, Western nations may need to redefine their approaches to international relations, embracing collaboration rather than competition as the basis for stability and progress.

A Convergence of Cultures and Philosophies

Baba Vanga's vision of East meeting West extended beyond political and economic power to include a profound cultural and intellectual exchange. She foresaw a blending of Eastern and Western philosophies, as people worldwide become more open to diverse perspectives and approaches to life. This convergence, she believed, would foster a greater appreciation for values such as balance, mindfulness, and interconnectedness—principles deeply rooted in Eastern traditions.

Her prophecy also included a revival of interest in Western principles such as individual rights and scientific inquiry, integrated into an emerging global consciousness that values both collective well-being and personal freedom. Baba Vanga's vision suggests that this blending of Eastern and Western perspectives could inspire humanity to tackle global issues with fresh insights and a holistic approach.

The Role of Technology in Bridging East and West

Baba Vanga foresaw technology playing a pivotal role in uniting East and West, enabling collaboration across borders and fostering cultural exchange. She envisioned digital platforms and communication tools that connect people, organizations, and governments, making it easier to share knowledge, resources, and solutions to global challenges. Her prophecy highlighted the potential of technology to facilitate understanding, reduce stereotypes, and build bridges between cultures.

At the same time, Baba Vanga warned of the potential for technology to create divisions if used to spread misinformation or promote political agendas. Her vision challenges humanity to leverage technology responsibly, ensuring that it serves as a tool for unity rather than division.

Shared Challenges and Collaborative Solutions

Baba Vanga believed that the convergence of East and West would be driven, in part, by shared global challenges that require collective action. She foresaw issues such as climate change, resource scarcity, and public health crises compelling nations to work together, pooling their knowledge and resources to develop sustainable solutions.

Her vision included Eastern nations contributing their expertise in renewable energy, conservation, and holistic health, while Western nations bring innovations in science, governance, and humanitarian efforts. This collaboration, she predicted, would create a stronger, more resilient global community capable of addressing complex issues. Baba Vanga's prophecy emphasizes the importance of viewing global challenges as shared responsibilities, fostering an ethos of cooperation rather than competition.

The Shift in Economic Power

A key aspect of Baba Vanga's prophecy was the shift in economic power from West to East. She foresaw Asian economies growing at unprecedented rates, supported by technological advancements, strategic investments, and growing consumer markets. Her vision included Eastern nations establishing new economic alliances, strengthening trade networks, and becoming major players in industries like technology, finance, and manufacturing.

This shift, she believed, would redefine global trade dynamics and influence how resources are allocated and managed. Baba Vanga's prediction suggests that by 2025, economic power will be more widely distributed, making international cooperation crucial to maintaining stability and prosperity in a multipolar world.

Challenges of East-West Collaboration

While Baba Vanga's prophecy was hopeful, she also acknowledged the challenges involved in fostering East-West collaboration. She foresaw potential conflicts over resources, values, and political ideologies, as nations navigate differences in governance, human rights, and economic priorities. Her vision emphasized the importance of diplomacy, cultural sensitivity, and a willingness to compromise in overcoming these obstacles.

Her prophecy also highlighted the potential for nationalistic sentiments to impede collaboration. Baba Vanga believed that humanity would need to rise above individual interests, recognizing that mutual respect and cooperation are essential for achieving shared goals. Her vision challenges nations to prioritize the common good, balancing sovereignty with the pursuit of global harmony.

The Emergence of a New Global Ethic

Baba Vanga foresaw the East-West convergence inspiring the development of a new global ethic, where principles of empathy, equity, and respect guide international relations. She believed that this ethic would shape policies on issues ranging from environmental stewardship to human rights, encouraging nations to act in the interest of future generations and the planet.

Her vision included the rise of leaders who embody these values, advocating for inclusive and responsible governance that benefits people across all regions. Baba Vanga's prophecy suggests that by 2025, humanity could begin to embrace a collective moral framework that transcends borders and promotes peace and prosperity for all.

Lessons from Baba Vanga's Prophecy

Baba Vanga's predictions about the global power shift offer several key lessons for navigating this transition:

- **Embrace Multipolarity:** Recognizing the benefits of a balanced distribution of power can foster a more cooperative and stable global community.
- **Promote Cultural Exchange:** Engaging with diverse perspectives enriches understanding and fosters mutual respect between East and West.
- **Leverage Technology for Unity:** Using technology to facilitate communication and collaboration can bridge cultural divides and create shared solutions.
- **Prioritize Shared Goals:** Focusing on common challenges, such as climate change and public health, encourages nations to work together for the collective good.
- **Support Ethical Leadership:** Elevating leaders who prioritize empathy, equity, and global responsibility can guide humanity through complex transitions.

Hope for a Harmonious Future

Baba Vanga's vision of East meeting West is ultimately one of hope and unity. She believed that humanity's strength lies in its diversity and that by embracing different perspectives, cultures, and strengths, the world can build a more inclusive and resilient future. Her prophecy suggests that while the transition may be challenging, the rewards of cooperation and mutual respect are immense.

As we continue to explore her predictions, Baba Vanga's insights inspire us to approach the future with openness, curiosity, and a commitment to building bridges across divides. Her vision reminds us that in an interconnected world, collaboration is essential, and that the convergence of East and West offers an opportunity to create a world that reflects humanity's highest values and aspirations.

The Digital Economy and Cryptocurrency Predictions

Baba Vanga's visions for 2025 included intriguing insights into the rise of the digital economy and the transformative role of cryptocurrencies. She foresaw a world where traditional financial systems would be increasingly replaced by digital platforms, allowing people to transact, save, and invest through decentralized technologies. Her prophecy suggested that cryptocurrencies and blockchain-based assets would play a pivotal role in reshaping economies, fostering financial inclusion, and challenging conventional banking structures. This chapter delves into Baba Vanga's predictions for the digital economy, the evolution of cryptocurrencies, and the impact these changes could have on individuals and global markets.

The Rise of the Digital Economy

Baba Vanga foresaw a shift from cash-based and traditional banking systems to a digital-first economy. She envisioned a world where digital platforms allow for instant transactions, efficient international transfers, and a seamless marketplace for goods and services. In her prophecy, the digital economy empowers individuals by reducing reliance on banks, offering greater financial freedom, and democratizing access to financial services.

This prediction aligns with current trends, as e-commerce, digital payments, and online banking have become integral to daily life. Baba Vanga's vision suggests that by 2025, digital transactions will dominate the global economy, with more people embracing digital wallets, online payment apps, and peer-to-peer lending platforms.

Cryptocurrencies as the New Standard

According to Baba Vanga's prophecy, cryptocurrencies would become a fundamental part of the global financial system, gradually replacing or complementing traditional fiat currencies. She foresaw cryptocurrencies like Bitcoin and Ethereum gaining widespread acceptance, with businesses, governments, and individuals adopting them for transactions, investments, and savings.

Her vision included the development of a stable, universally accepted digital currency that transcends national borders, creating a truly global economy. This aligns with current conversations about central bank digital currencies (CBDCs) and stablecoins, which aim to offer the stability of fiat currency with the efficiency and transparency of digital assets. Baba Vanga's prophecy suggests that in 2025, cryptocurrencies could become the new standard for transactions, bridging financial gaps and enhancing economic resilience.

The Role of Blockchain Technology

Baba Vanga foresaw blockchain technology playing a crucial role in enabling the digital economy. She believed that its decentralized, transparent, and secure nature would revolutionize industries beyond finance, including supply chain management, real estate, healthcare, and voting systems. Her vision emphasized blockchain's potential to create trust in digital transactions, reduce fraud, and improve accountability across various sectors.

Her prophecy aligns with current innovations in blockchain, where companies are exploring ways to use the technology for everything from tracking goods to verifying identities. Baba Vanga's prediction suggests that by 2025, blockchain could become a foundational technology for numerous industries, creating a more transparent and efficient global economy.

Financial Inclusion and Empowerment

One of Baba Vanga's most hopeful predictions about the digital economy is its potential to promote financial inclusion. She foresaw digital currencies and decentralized finance (DeFi) platforms providing financial services to people in underserved regions, where traditional banking infrastructure is limited. Her vision included mobile banking, digital wallets, and peer-to-peer lending becoming accessible to millions, helping them save, invest, and participate in the economy.

This aspect of her prophecy highlights the democratizing power of digital finance, enabling people worldwide to gain financial independence and stability. Baba Vanga believed that the digital economy would empower individuals by giving them direct control over their assets, reducing reliance on intermediaries, and creating opportunities for economic mobility.

Challenges and Risks of the Digital Economy

While Baba Vanga was optimistic about the rise of the digital economy, she also warned of potential risks and challenges. She foresaw issues such as cybercrime, fraud, and market volatility as threats to digital assets. Her vision emphasized the need for strong cybersecurity measures, regulatory oversight, and education to protect users and ensure a stable financial environment.

Her prophecy also highlighted concerns about inequality in digital access. She foresaw that people in remote or under-resourced areas might struggle to participate in the digital economy due to lack of internet connectivity, digital literacy, or access to devices. Baba Vanga's vision challenges policymakers and technology companies to address these disparities, ensuring that the benefits of the digital economy are accessible to everyone.

Regulation and Government Involvement

Baba Vanga predicted that governments would play an increasingly active role in regulating the digital economy and cryptocurrencies. She foresaw a delicate balance between supporting innovation and protecting consumers, with governments introducing policies to prevent fraud, stabilize markets, and ensure compliance with financial standards. Her vision included the emergence of central bank digital currencies (CBDCs), which combine the efficiency of digital currencies with the backing of national governments.

Her prophecy also suggested that some governments might initially resist the rise of decentralized cryptocurrencies, seeing them as a threat to traditional banking and monetary policy. However, she believed that collaboration and adaptation would eventually prevail, as governments recognize the benefits of a well-regulated digital economy. Baba Vanga's vision suggests that by 2025, regulatory frameworks for cryptocurrencies and digital finance could become more standardized globally, fostering trust and stability.

The Social Impact of Digital Finance

Baba Vanga foresaw the digital economy affecting social structures, as financial transactions become more seamless, transparent, and accessible. She believed that digital finance would empower individuals by offering greater control over personal finances and creating opportunities for entrepreneurship, particularly among younger generations. Her vision included digital platforms enabling microloans, crowdfunding, and small business growth, contributing to local economies and fostering a spirit of innovation.

At the same time, she warned of the potential for social disruptions if people become overly reliant on digital wealth, emphasizing the importance of financial education and responsible investment. Baba Vanga's prophecy suggests that while digital finance offers new opportunities, a balanced approach is essential for sustainable growth.

The Future of Work in a Digital Economy

Baba Vanga's predictions also touched on the impact of the digital economy on work and employment. She foresaw an increase in remote work, gig economies, and decentralized organizations enabled by digital platforms and blockchain technology. In her vision, more people would be able to work independently, leveraging skills across borders and creating new career paths.

This aspect of her prophecy reflects the current rise of the digital workforce, where people increasingly rely on technology to work, collaborate, and innovate. Baba Vanga's vision suggests that by 2025, traditional employment structures could evolve to accommodate the flexibility and autonomy offered by the digital economy, enabling a new era of work that aligns with individual needs and global opportunities.

Lessons from Baba Vanga's Prophecy

Baba Vanga's predictions about the digital economy and cryptocurrency offer several key lessons for navigating this transformation:

- **Promote Financial Inclusion:** Ensuring that digital finance is accessible to everyone is essential for a fair and inclusive economy.
- **Support Responsible Innovation:** Embracing blockchain and cryptocurrencies while establishing safeguards can help protect users and create stability.
- **Strengthen Cybersecurity:** Investing in robust security measures is critical to building trust and resilience in the digital economy.
- **Balance Regulation and Freedom:** Governments should foster innovation while implementing frameworks that protect consumers and stabilize markets.
- **Educate and Empower Users:** Financial literacy and awareness of digital risks are essential to navigating the new economy responsibly.

Hope for an Inclusive Financial Future

Baba Vanga's vision of the digital economy is ultimately one of empowerment and possibility. She believed that the rise of digital finance and cryptocurrencies would enable people to gain greater control over their financial lives, creating a more inclusive and resilient global economy. Her prophecy challenges us to approach these innovations with foresight, responsibility, and a commitment to ensuring that their benefits reach everyone.

As we continue exploring her predictions, Baba Vanga's insights inspire us to embrace the digital transformation while addressing its challenges, fostering a financial system that reflects humanity's highest ideals of equity, transparency, and opportunity. Her vision reminds us that the digital economy has the potential to unlock new avenues for progress, bringing the world closer to a future where financial freedom and security are within reach for all.

The Impact of Climate Refugees: A Humanitarian Crisis?

Baba Vanga's predictions for 2025 included a stark vision of the human impact of climate change, particularly the rise of climate refugees—people forced to leave their homes due to environmental disasters, rising sea levels, and resource scarcity. She foresaw millions displaced by events such as droughts, floods, and wildfires, sparking a humanitarian crisis that would strain resources, infrastructure, and international relations. This chapter explores her vision of climate refugees, examining the causes, potential consequences, and the moral imperative for global action to address this pressing issue.

The Drivers of Climate Displacement

Baba Vanga's prophecy identified several environmental factors driving the rise of climate refugees. She foresaw regions experiencing more frequent and severe natural disasters, such as hurricanes, floods, and droughts, making it increasingly difficult for people to live safely in vulnerable areas. Her vision also included rising sea levels that threaten coastal communities, forcing residents to relocate inland.

These challenges align with current scientific projections, which warn of the significant impacts climate change will have on habitable land. Baba Vanga's prediction suggests that by 2025, the acceleration of these environmental shifts could push many communities to a tipping point, making displacement an unavoidable reality for millions.

Resource Scarcity and Conflict

In addition to natural disasters, Baba Vanga foresaw resource scarcity as a key driver of displacement, with people leaving regions where water, food, and arable land become increasingly scarce. Her vision included images of communities competing for diminishing resources, sparking conflict and instability. She believed that climate-related resource scarcity would contribute to social and political tensions, increasing the likelihood of regional conflicts over access to essential resources.

Her prophecy underscores the importance of managing resources sustainably and equitably. Baba Vanga's vision suggests that without proactive measures to address scarcity, regions affected by climate change could experience destabilizing competition, leading to an escalating crisis of displacement and conflict.

The Global Humanitarian Crisis

Baba Vanga's prophecy depicted the displacement of climate refugees as a humanitarian crisis that would extend beyond national borders, affecting countries worldwide. She foresaw waves of displaced individuals and families seeking refuge in safer regions, overwhelming host countries and challenging their capacity to provide shelter, healthcare, and basic necessities.

Her vision resonates with current concerns about the limits of humanitarian resources, as existing refugee systems are already strained by conflicts and economic migrations. Baba Vanga's prophecy suggests that by 2025, the scale of climate displacement could push humanitarian organizations and host countries to their limits, requiring a coordinated global response to ensure that the needs of climate refugees are met with compassion and efficiency.

The Economic Impact of Climate Displacement

Baba Vanga predicted that climate displacement would also have significant economic consequences for both displaced individuals and host countries. She foresaw disruptions to local economies, as people leave regions where agriculture and industry are no longer viable. At the same time, she believed that host countries could experience economic strain due to the costs associated with accommodating large numbers of refugees.

However, her vision also included the potential for positive economic contributions from refugees, who bring skills, labor, and cultural diversity to their new communities. Baba Vanga's prophecy suggests that while climate displacement poses economic challenges, proactive policies that integrate refugees into local economies can help mitigate these effects and create opportunities for growth and development.

Health and Social Challenges

Baba Vanga foresaw that the climate refugee crisis would bring a host of health and social challenges. She envisioned refugee populations facing increased risks of infectious diseases due to overcrowded living conditions and limited access to healthcare. Mental health issues, including trauma from displacement and loss, were also a concern in her vision, as climate refugees struggle to adjust to their new circumstances and cope with the stress of starting over.

Her prophecy emphasizes the importance of providing comprehensive support for climate refugees, including healthcare, education, and mental health services. Baba Vanga believed that addressing these challenges is essential for helping displaced individuals and communities regain stability and dignity in their new environments.

Moral and Ethical Imperatives

Baba Vanga's vision of the climate refugee crisis included a strong moral and ethical dimension, urging humanity to respond with empathy, responsibility, and compassion. She believed that climate refugees are among the most vulnerable members of society, often bearing the brunt of environmental changes they did not cause. Her prophecy challenged nations to recognize their shared responsibility to protect and support those affected by climate displacement.

Her vision underscores the importance of international solidarity and cooperation, suggesting that wealthier nations have an ethical duty to assist countries most impacted by climate change. Baba Vanga's prophecy encourages humanity to view climate refugees not as a burden, but as people deserving of respect, support, and a chance to rebuild their lives with dignity.

The Role of International Policy and Cooperation

Baba Vanga foresaw the need for international cooperation in addressing the climate refugee crisis. She envisioned global frameworks that provide clear guidelines for the protection, relocation, and integration of climate refugees. In her vision, countries worked together to create sustainable solutions, sharing resources, expertise, and financial support to ease the strain on host nations.

Her prophecy aligns with calls for the establishment of legal protections for climate refugees, as current international frameworks often exclude people displaced by environmental factors. Baba Vanga's vision suggests that by 2025, the international community must take meaningful steps toward recognizing climate refugees and creating policies that address their unique needs.

Adaptation and Resilience Strategies

While her vision acknowledged the inevitability of some displacement, Baba Vanga also believed that investment in adaptation and resilience could reduce the scale of the crisis. She foresaw communities implementing strategies to mitigate climate impacts, such as building infrastructure to protect against flooding, diversifying crops to withstand drought, and improving water management systems.

Her prophecy encourages nations to invest in resilience measures that allow communities to remain in place safely, reducing the need for displacement. Baba Vanga's vision suggests that by focusing on adaptation, countries can better protect vulnerable populations and prevent a large-scale refugee crisis.

Lessons from Baba Vanga's Prophecy

Baba Vanga's predictions about climate refugees and the humanitarian crisis they face offer several key lessons for global action:

- **Invest in Adaptation:** Strengthening resilience measures in vulnerable regions can help communities withstand environmental changes and reduce displacement.
- **Promote Global Cooperation:** Addressing the climate refugee crisis requires international solidarity, sharing resources, and coordinating policies to ensure equitable support.
- **Prioritize Humanitarian Aid:** Providing healthcare, shelter, and essential services is critical for supporting climate refugees and helping them rebuild their lives.
- **Integrate Refugees Economically:** Policies that allow refugees to contribute to their new communities can create mutual benefits and foster social integration.
- **Acknowledge Ethical Responsibilities:** Recognizing the moral imperative to support climate refugees is essential for building a compassionate, responsible global society.

Hope for a Compassionate Response

Baba Vanga's vision of climate refugees is a call for humanity to respond with compassion, dignity, and shared responsibility. She believed that while the climate refugee crisis presents significant challenges, it also offers an opportunity for nations to demonstrate their commitment to human rights and social justice. Her prophecy challenges us to address this issue with empathy and resilience, building systems that protect the most vulnerable and promote collective well-being.

As we continue to explore her predictions, Baba Vanga's insights inspire us to take proactive steps to support climate refugees and create a future where all people can live with security, dignity, and hope. Her vision reminds us that the true measure of humanity lies in how we care for one another, especially in times of crisis, and that by working together, we can build a more inclusive and compassionate world.

Nuclear Tensions and the Threat of a New Arms Race

Baba Vanga's predictions for 2025 included a sobering warning about rising nuclear tensions and the potential for a renewed arms race. She foresaw a world where geopolitical conflicts, fueled by competition and mistrust, spark a dangerous buildup of nuclear weapons. Her prophecy warned that without global cooperation and commitment to disarmament, humanity could face heightened risks of conflict and catastrophic consequences. This chapter explores her vision of nuclear tensions, the drivers of an arms race, and the urgent need for diplomacy and peace-building to prevent a global crisis.

The Resurgence of Nuclear Tensions

Baba Vanga foresaw a resurgence in nuclear tensions by 2025, as nations respond to perceived threats by increasing their military capabilities. She envisioned countries investing in advanced weapons technologies, seeking to assert dominance or deter rivals. Her prophecy described a world where nuclear weapons, once seen as a last resort, become central to defense strategies, leading to an atmosphere of anxiety and fear.

This vision aligns with current trends, as major powers modernize their nuclear arsenals, and smaller nations pursue nuclear capabilities. Baba Vanga's prophecy warns of the destabilizing effects of this buildup, suggesting that renewed nuclear tensions could erode decades of progress in arms control and increase the likelihood of accidents or miscalculations.

Drivers of a New Arms Race

Baba Vanga identified several factors fueling the potential for a new nuclear arms race. Central to her prophecy was the growing competition among major powers, each seeking to protect its interests and assert influence. She foresaw conflicts over resources, territorial claims, and ideological differences driving nations to expand their arsenals as a show of strength.

Her vision also highlighted technological advancements, such as hypersonic missiles and cyber warfare capabilities, as additional factors intensifying the arms race. With the development of new weapons that can evade traditional defenses, Baba Vanga predicted that nations would feel pressured to keep up, resulting in a dangerous escalation cycle. Her prophecy underscores the need for international frameworks to regulate these technologies and prevent an unchecked arms race.

The Erosion of Arms Control Agreements

Baba Vanga foresaw the weakening of arms control agreements that had previously helped limit nuclear proliferation and promote stability. She believed that the erosion of these treaties would remove important safeguards, making it easier for nations to develop and deploy nuclear weapons. Her prophecy included images of negotiations breaking down, with distrust and political maneuvering hindering efforts to reach new agreements.

This aspect of her vision resonates with current concerns about the decline of arms control agreements, such as the Intermediate-Range Nuclear Forces (INF) Treaty and the New START Treaty, which have faced challenges in recent years. Baba Vanga's prediction suggests that without renewed commitment to arms control, humanity risks returning to a state of unchecked proliferation, where the pursuit of nuclear superiority could lead to devastating consequences.

The Risk of Nuclear Conflict and Accidents

Baba Vanga warned that the escalation of nuclear tensions increases the risk of conflict and accidents, with potentially catastrophic consequences. She foresaw scenarios where miscommunication, technological failures, or human error could lead to unintended escalation, sparking a conflict that neither side desires. Her vision included images of near-misses and moments of crisis, where the world stands on the brink of disaster.

Her prophecy serves as a reminder of the inherent risks of nuclear weapons, which require high levels of control, communication, and caution to prevent unintended use. Baba Vanga's vision emphasizes the importance of clear protocols, transparency, and diplomacy in managing nuclear capabilities, reducing the risk of accidental or miscalculated actions that could lead to widespread destruction.

The Role of Diplomacy and Peace-Building

While Baba Vanga's vision of nuclear tensions was concerning, she also believed in the power of diplomacy and peace-building to prevent escalation. She foresaw a role for international organizations, peace advocates, and diplomatic leaders in de-escalating tensions and promoting dialogue. In her prophecy, nations come together to address their differences and seek mutually beneficial solutions, recognizing that cooperation is essential for global security.

Her vision highlighted the importance of trust-building measures, such as transparent arms inspections, regular communication channels, and conflict resolution mechanisms. Baba Vanga believed that diplomacy and open dialogue could counteract the distrust driving nuclear tensions, paving the way for agreements that prioritize peace and stability.

The Ethical Implications of Nuclear Weapons

Baba Vanga's prophecy included a reflection on the ethical implications of nuclear weapons, urging humanity to consider the moral responsibility of possessing such destructive power. She believed that the continued existence of nuclear arsenals posed a threat to humanity's survival, emphasizing that the risks far outweigh any strategic advantages.

Her vision challenged nations to rethink the purpose of nuclear weapons, advocating for a world where security is achieved through cooperation and trust rather than deterrence and fear. Baba Vanga's prophecy calls for a global re-evaluation of nuclear policies, encouraging nations to pursue disarmament and shift their focus toward sustainable peace.

The Movement for Nuclear Disarmament

Baba Vanga foresaw the rise of a global movement advocating for nuclear disarmament, with citizens, activists, and leaders working together to eliminate nuclear threats. She envisioned communities mobilizing to demand reductions in nuclear arsenals, pressuring governments to prioritize disarmament and reinvest in peace-building efforts. Her prophecy suggested that by 2025, this movement could gain momentum, inspiring a renewed commitment to reducing nuclear risks.

This vision aligns with contemporary disarmament initiatives, such as the Treaty on the Prohibition of Nuclear Weapons (TPNW), which seeks to ban nuclear weapons and promote non-proliferation. Baba Vanga's prophecy suggests that a growing public awareness of nuclear dangers could lead to greater support for disarmament, fostering a global shift away from nuclear reliance.

The Need for Education and Awareness

Baba Vanga believed that raising public awareness about the risks of nuclear weapons is essential for preventing an arms race. Her prophecy emphasized the importance of educating people about the consequences of nuclear conflict, the ethical issues surrounding nuclear deterrence, and the benefits of disarmament. She foresaw educational campaigns, documentaries, and public discussions sparking a shift in public opinion, creating a groundswell of support for policies that prioritize peace and security.

Her vision challenges governments, educators, and activists to foster a culture of awareness and responsibility, empowering people to advocate for a world free from nuclear threats. Baba Vanga's prophecy suggests that by cultivating a well-informed public, humanity can influence policy decisions and reduce the likelihood of an arms race.

Lessons from Baba Vanga's Prophecy

Baba Vanga's predictions about nuclear tensions and the threat of a new arms race offer several key lessons for fostering global security:

- **Renew Commitment to Arms Control:** Strengthening and updating arms control agreements is essential for limiting nuclear proliferation and promoting stability.
- **Invest in Diplomacy:** Encouraging dialogue and trust-building measures can reduce tensions and prevent escalation, fostering a more secure world.
- **Support Disarmament Efforts:** Pursuing nuclear disarmament and reducing arsenals aligns with ethical responsibilities and reduces global risks.
- **Educate and Raise Awareness:** Informing the public about the dangers of nuclear weapons can create a movement for peace, influencing policy and promoting disarmament.
- **Promote Ethical Leadership:** Leaders who prioritize global security, empathy, and cooperation are essential for navigating complex nuclear issues.

Hope for a Peaceful Future

Baba Vanga's vision of nuclear tensions and the threat of an arms race is a call for humanity to choose a path of peace, responsibility, and cooperation. She believed that while the risks of nuclear conflict are significant, the power to prevent it lies within humanity's hands. Her prophecy challenges us to recognize the ethical and practical importance of disarmament, fostering a world where security is built on trust rather than fear.

As we continue to explore her predictions, Baba Vanga's insights remind us of the need for vigilance, diplomacy, and a shared commitment to peace. Her vision serves as a powerful call to action, inspiring humanity to work together to prevent nuclear escalation and build a future where all people can live in safety and harmony.

Baba Vanga on the Rise of New Superpowers

Baba Vanga's predictions for 2025 included a vision of emerging superpowers reshaping the global order. She foresaw a world where new nations and alliances rise to prominence, challenging traditional Western powers and creating a more multipolar world. Her prophecy suggested that these new superpowers would bring fresh perspectives and alternative approaches to governance, economy, and international relations. In this chapter, we explore Baba Vanga's vision of the rise of new superpowers, the factors driving their emergence, and the implications for global politics and society.

The Decline of Western Dominance

Baba Vanga predicted a shift away from Western dominance, with the influence of traditional powers such as the United States and European nations becoming less pronounced. She foresaw that while Western countries would remain influential, their role in global affairs would gradually diminish as other nations gain power and assert their presence on the world stage. Her prophecy suggests that by 2025, the balance of power will be more evenly distributed, with Western nations adjusting to a new, more competitive geopolitical landscape.

This prediction aligns with recent shifts in global dynamics, where economic, technological, and political growth in regions outside the West—particularly in Asia, the Middle East, and parts of Africa—are challenging long-standing power structures. Baba Vanga's vision suggests that adapting to this new balance will require Western nations to prioritize diplomacy and cooperation over competition.

The Rise of China and India

Baba Vanga identified China and India as prominent players in the new global order, predicting that they would become superpowers capable of rivaling Western influence. She foresaw China asserting its economic and technological strength, extending its reach through initiatives such as the Belt and Road Initiative, which connects Asia, Africa, and Europe through infrastructure and trade networks. Her vision included China's advancements in technology, space exploration, and renewable energy, positioning it as a formidable global leader.

Similarly, she predicted India's rise, foreseeing its economic expansion, technological advancements, and increasing influence in regional and global affairs. India's youthful population and robust tech sector, she believed, would fuel its growth, allowing it to play a central role in shaping policies on issues such as climate change, digital innovation, and healthcare. Baba Vanga's vision suggests that by 2025, China and India could form the core of a new geopolitical axis, balancing and, in some areas, surpassing Western influence.

The Emergence of Regional Powers

Beyond China and India, Baba Vanga foresaw the rise of regional powers that would influence their respective regions and beyond. She envisioned nations in the Middle East, Africa, and Latin America stepping into leadership roles, advocating for their interests on the global stage and forming alliances to counterbalance traditional superpowers.

In her prophecy, countries such as Brazil, South Africa, Nigeria, and Saudi Arabia play critical roles in shaping economic and political agendas within their regions, each bringing unique resources, cultural strengths, and geopolitical influence. Baba Vanga believed that these emerging regional powers would promote diverse perspectives and push for policies that reflect their interests and values, contributing to a multipolar world where no single nation or bloc holds absolute dominance.

New Alliances and Strategic Partnerships

Baba Vanga's prophecy included the formation of new alliances and strategic partnerships, as nations recognize the importance of collaboration in addressing global challenges. She foresaw alliances that cross traditional political and cultural divides, with nations coming together based on shared interests in areas like technology, climate action, and economic development.

In her vision, these alliances would prioritize mutual respect and cooperation, moving beyond the zero-sum thinking that has historically characterized international relations. Baba Vanga believed that by 2025, new alliances would emerge as influential players in global governance, advocating for policies that promote collective well-being and sustainable growth. Her prophecy emphasizes the importance of unity and cooperation, suggesting that these partnerships could help stabilize the world and foster peace.

The Role of Technology and Innovation

Baba Vanga predicted that technological advancements would be a driving force behind the rise of new superpowers. She foresaw nations investing heavily in fields such as artificial intelligence, biotechnology, space exploration, and renewable energy, positioning themselves as leaders in the industries of the future. In her prophecy, technology becomes a currency of power, with nations that excel in innovation gaining influence and competitive advantage.

This vision aligns with the current trend of countries investing in technology to bolster their economies and assert their presence on the global stage. Baba Vanga's prediction suggests that by 2025, technological leadership will be a key determinant of superpower status, with nations racing to develop and control transformative technologies.

Economic Resilience and Resource Management

Baba Vanga believed that economic resilience and sustainable resource management would be essential factors in the rise of new superpowers. She foresaw nations that effectively manage their natural resources, address environmental issues, and build robust economies emerging as global leaders. In her vision, these countries prioritize long-term stability over short-term gains, using their resources wisely and promoting sustainable development.

Her prophecy includes examples of nations that have diversified their economies and reduced dependence on foreign imports, thereby becoming more self-sufficient and resilient to global economic fluctuations. Baba Vanga's vision suggests that by 2025, nations with a focus on sustainability and resilience will gain respect and influence in the international community, setting a new standard for responsible leadership.

The Shift toward Multilateralism

Baba Vanga's vision of a multipolar world also included a shift toward multilateralism, where decisions are made collectively rather than unilaterally. She foresaw a renewed emphasis on international organizations, such as the United Nations and regional unions, to mediate conflicts, foster cooperation, and address global issues. Her prophecy emphasized that in a world with multiple superpowers, multilateralism would be essential for managing tensions and maintaining global stability.

In her vision, nations actively engage in dialogue and negotiation, working together to solve problems such as climate change, cybersecurity threats, and economic inequality. Baba Vanga believed that by embracing multilateralism, humanity could navigate the complexities of a multipolar world more effectively, promoting peace and progress for all.

Challenges and Potential Conflicts

While Baba Vanga's prophecy was optimistic about the rise of new superpowers, she also acknowledged the challenges and potential conflicts that could arise. She foresaw competition over resources, technological leadership, and influence as new powers assert themselves, leading to rivalries and tensions that could destabilize regions.

Her vision highlighted the risk of ideological clashes between nations with differing governance models, economic priorities, and cultural values. Baba Vanga's prophecy challenges leaders to approach these differences with diplomacy, recognizing that cooperation and mutual respect are essential for preventing conflicts and promoting a harmonious world.

The Role of Ethical Leadership

Baba Vanga believed that ethical leadership would be critical in shaping the future of a multipolar world. She foresaw a new generation of leaders emerging from these rising powers, individuals who prioritize inclusivity, transparency, and responsibility. Her prophecy suggested that these leaders would advocate for policies that reflect the needs and aspirations of their people, promoting social justice, environmental stewardship, and economic equity.

Her vision challenges nations to hold their leaders accountable and to choose individuals who are committed to ethical governance. Baba Vanga believed that only by fostering a culture of integrity and compassion can new superpowers create a positive impact on the global stage.

Lessons from Baba Vanga's Prophecy

Baba Vanga's predictions about the rise of new superpowers offer several key lessons for navigating this transformation:

- **Embrace Multipolarity:** Recognizing and respecting the diversity of power centers can foster a more stable and inclusive global order.
- **Promote Multilateralism:** Supporting international cooperation and collective decision-making is essential for addressing complex global challenges.
- **Invest in Sustainability:** Economic resilience and sustainable resource management are crucial for long-term stability and influence.
- **Encourage Ethical Leadership:** Leaders who prioritize transparency, inclusivity, and responsibility can help guide the world toward a more just and equitable future.
- **Foster Innovation and Collaboration:** Embracing technological advancements and cross-border partnerships can help nations thrive and contribute to global progress.

Hope for a Balanced Global Order

Baba Vanga's vision of new superpowers rising is ultimately one of hope for a more balanced, equitable world. She believed that the diversification of power could promote greater cooperation, inclusivity, and resilience, creating a global order that reflects humanity's shared values and aspirations. Her prophecy challenges us to welcome this transformation, embracing the opportunities and responsibilities that come with a multipolar world.

As we continue to explore her predictions, Baba Vanga's insights remind us that global power is not merely about dominance but about the ability to foster positive change. Her vision inspires us to support ethical governance, sustainable practices, and collaborative efforts, creating a future where all nations can contribute to a world of peace, prosperity, and harmony.

Technological Utopia or Dystopia: Baba Vanga's Insights

Baba Vanga's visions for 2025 included profound insights into humanity's relationship with technology, offering glimpses of both utopian and dystopian outcomes. She foresaw a world where rapid advancements in artificial intelligence, robotics, virtual reality, and biotechnology could either elevate society to new heights or create unforeseen dangers and ethical dilemmas. According to her prophecy, whether technology serves as a force for good or harm depends largely on how humanity approaches its development, regulation, and integration. This chapter explores Baba Vanga's vision of a potential technological utopia or dystopia, examining the factors that could lead humanity down one path or the other.

The Promise of a Technological Utopia

Baba Vanga envisioned a utopian scenario where technology brings profound benefits, improving the quality of life for people around the world. She foresaw advancements in medicine, AI, and clean energy creating a world where diseases are cured, poverty is reduced, and sustainable energy is widely available. Her vision of a technological utopia included:

- **Medical Breakthroughs:** Baba Vanga predicted that technology would revolutionize healthcare, with cures for previously untreatable diseases, personalized medicine, and innovations like regenerative treatments and artificial organs. This would allow people to live longer, healthier lives, with improved access to affordable healthcare.
- **Sustainable Energy Solutions:** She foresaw advancements in renewable energy technologies, such as solar, wind, and fusion power, enabling humanity to transition away from fossil fuels. In her vision, clean energy becomes accessible to all, reducing environmental degradation and creating a sustainable foundation for the future.
- **Education and Knowledge Accessibility:** Baba Vanga predicted a world where technology democratizes education, making knowledge freely available to people across the globe. In her vision, online platforms, virtual classrooms, and AI-driven learning tools provide opportunities for individuals to develop skills, pursue careers, and contribute to society.
- **Enhanced Quality of Life:** Her prophecy included AI and automation reducing the burden of repetitive and dangerous tasks, allowing people to focus on creative and meaningful pursuits. She envisioned technology supporting human potential, empowering individuals to achieve a higher quality of life and fostering a culture of innovation, collaboration, and personal fulfillment.

The Threat of a Technological Dystopia

While Baba Vanga was hopeful about technology's potential, she also warned of a dystopian outcome where technology could lead to control, inequality, and loss of human autonomy. Her vision of a technological dystopia included:

- **Surveillance and Loss of Privacy:** Baba Vanga foresaw the rise of surveillance technologies, with AI and data analytics enabling governments and corporations to monitor people's movements, communications, and behaviors. She warned of the risks of a society where privacy becomes a luxury, and individuals lose control over their personal information.

- **Unemployment and Economic Inequality:** Her prophecy included the widespread automation of jobs, potentially displacing workers and creating economic disparity. While automation could free people from mundane tasks, she warned that it could also lead to increased unemployment and social inequality if societies fail to adapt and provide support for displaced workers.
- **Social Isolation and Mental Health Challenges:** Baba Vanga foresaw a society where digital platforms, virtual reality, and social media could lead to social isolation, addiction, and a decline in mental well-being. She warned of the dangers of people losing touch with real-world relationships and becoming overly reliant on virtual interactions.
- **Loss of Human Autonomy:** Her prophecy also included concerns about AI becoming too powerful, with autonomous systems making decisions that impact human lives. Baba Vanga warned of a future where humanity could lose control over AI and technology, creating a scenario where machines operate beyond human oversight or moral accountability.

The Role of Artificial Intelligence

Baba Vanga's prophecy placed particular emphasis on artificial intelligence as a pivotal force in shaping the future. She foresaw AI becoming deeply integrated into society, with applications in healthcare, education, security, and even government decision-making. Her vision suggested that AI could either serve as a tool for human empowerment or become a source of control, depending on how it is designed and regulated.

She warned of the potential for AI to surpass human intelligence, leading to an imbalance of power. Baba Vanga believed that if humanity does not set clear ethical guidelines and oversight, AI could create unintended consequences that challenge human autonomy. Her prophecy suggests that the responsible development of AI is crucial to ensuring that it serves humanity rather than controlling it.

The Ethical Dilemmas of Biotechnology

Baba Vanga foresaw biotechnology as another area with profound potential and ethical challenges. She predicted breakthroughs in genetic engineering, cloning, and neural enhancements, offering humanity the chance to overcome physical limitations and eliminate genetic diseases. However, she also warned of the ethical dilemmas associated with these technologies, particularly the risk of creating inequality or commodifying human life.

Her vision included debates about the acceptable limits of genetic manipulation, raising questions about the potential for "designer" traits and the impact on social dynamics. Baba Vanga believed that humanity must approach biotechnology with caution, considering the moral implications and ensuring that advancements benefit society as a whole rather than creating new forms of division.

The Need for Ethical Leadership and Regulation

Baba Vanga's prophecy underscored the importance of ethical leadership and regulatory frameworks in guiding technology's development. She believed that clear guidelines, oversight, and accountability are essential for ensuring that technology serves humanity's best interests. Her vision called for leaders who prioritize social well-being over profit, recognizing the potential risks of unchecked technological growth.

In her vision, Baba Vanga emphasized the role of international cooperation in regulating emerging technologies. She foresaw the need for global agreements on AI, cybersecurity, and biotechnology, recognizing that these technologies have cross-border impacts and require collective responsibility. Her prophecy challenges leaders to work together to create a framework for responsible innovation, balancing progress with caution.

Education and Technological Literacy

Baba Vanga believed that education would play a vital role in shaping humanity's approach to technology. She foresaw a world where technological literacy becomes essential, enabling people to understand, interact with, and critically assess new technologies. In her vision, education empowers individuals to navigate the digital landscape, protecting themselves from exploitation and understanding the ethical dimensions of technological advancements.

Her prophecy also suggested that fostering critical thinking and ethical awareness would be crucial in a world shaped by technology. Baba Vanga believed that by educating individuals on the potential benefits and risks of technology, society could make informed choices that support a utopian future rather than a dystopian one.

Balancing Humanity and Technology

Baba Vanga's prophecy stressed the importance of maintaining a balance between humanity and technology. She warned against becoming overly dependent on machines, emphasizing that true progress involves using technology to enhance human potential, not replace it. Her vision called for a future where technology serves as a tool for empowerment, fostering creativity, connection, and growth while preserving human values and autonomy.

Baba Vanga believed that humanity must remain rooted in compassion, ethics, and shared responsibility. Her prophecy challenges us to remember that technological advancements are only as beneficial as the values guiding them, and that humanity's role is to shape technology in ways that uplift rather than diminish.

Lessons from Baba Vanga's Prophecy

Baba Vanga's insights on the potential for a technological utopia or dystopia offer several key lessons for navigating this transformation:

- **Prioritize Ethical Development:** Focusing on responsible and ethical development can help ensure that technology serves humanity's best interests.
- **Educate and Empower the Public:** Technological literacy and critical thinking are essential for individuals to make informed decisions and understand the ethical implications of technology.
- **Promote International Cooperation:** Collaborative regulation and shared responsibility can address global challenges posed by AI, biotechnology, and other emerging technologies.
- **Balance Innovation with Humanity:** Ensuring that technology supports human values, autonomy, and well-being is essential for creating a utopian future.
- **Foster Ethical Leadership:** Leaders who prioritize social good, transparency, and long-term consequences can guide humanity toward a harmonious relationship with technology.

Hope for a Harmonious Future with Technology

Baba Vanga's vision of a technological utopia or dystopia reminds us of the dual nature of innovation. While technology has the potential to transform society positively, it also brings challenges that require thoughtful regulation and ethical consideration. Her prophecy inspires hope for a future where technology enhances human life and uplifts society, but also cautions us to remain vigilant and responsible. As we continue exploring her predictions, Baba Vanga's insights encourage us to approach technology with wisdom and balance, recognizing that the path to a utopian future lies in our commitment to guiding innovation in ways that honor human dignity, ethics, and shared well-being.

Energy Wars: The Battle for Resources in 2025

Baba Vanga's predictions for 2025 included a vision of escalating competition for energy resources, a trend she saw as a potential trigger for conflict between nations. She foresaw that as global demand for energy rises, countries may find themselves increasingly vying for access to critical resources like oil, natural gas, and rare minerals essential for renewable technologies. Her prophecy warned that without sustainable and equitable approaches to resource management, humanity could face a series of "energy wars" that destabilize regions and threaten international security. In this chapter, we explore Baba Vanga's vision of energy-driven conflicts, the factors fueling them, and the potential pathways for peaceful cooperation in resource sharing.

The Growing Demand for Energy

Baba Vanga foresaw that as the global population grows and economies expand, the demand for energy will reach unprecedented levels by 2025. She envisioned an energy landscape in which countries require more power to fuel urban growth, industrial development, and technological advancement. Her prophecy included an intensified scramble for both fossil fuels and the minerals essential for clean energy technologies, such as lithium, cobalt, and rare earth elements used in batteries, solar panels, and wind turbines.

Her prediction aligns with contemporary concerns about resource scarcity, as the energy needs of emerging economies converge with those of established industrialized nations. Baba Vanga's vision suggests that without a shift towards sustainable and collaborative energy solutions, the competition for resources could lead to heightened tensions and a struggle for dominance over energy supply chains.

The Shift towards Renewable Energy and New Dependencies

Baba Vanga predicted that while countries would increasingly shift toward renewable energy to mitigate climate change, this transition would bring its own set of challenges and dependencies. She foresaw that the demand for renewable technologies would drive up the need for specific minerals and materials, many of which are concentrated in only a few regions of the world. Her vision included potential conflicts over access to these resources, as nations secure supplies to support their renewable energy ambitions.

This aspect of her prophecy highlights a paradox of the green energy transition: while renewable energy reduces dependency on fossil fuels, it creates new dependencies on rare materials, many of which are controlled by a limited number of countries. Baba Vanga's prediction suggests that by 2025, these new dependencies could become sources of conflict, especially if resource-rich nations use their control over these materials as leverage in geopolitical negotiations.

Geopolitical Tensions and Strategic Control

Baba Vanga foresaw nations increasingly viewing energy resources as assets of strategic importance, leading to a geopolitical landscape marked by competition and power plays. She predicted that countries would form alliances, negotiate exclusive access agreements, and even resort to coercion or military intervention to secure critical resources. Her vision included regions like the Middle East, Central Asia, and Africa becoming focal points of international interest due to their abundance of oil, gas, and minerals.

In her prophecy, Baba Vanga highlighted the risk of "energy blocs" forming, with countries banding together to control resource flows and influence global energy markets. This vision aligns with modern trends, where energy independence and control over supply chains are central to national security strategies. Baba Vanga's prediction suggests that without collaborative policies, these competitive dynamics could lead to a fragile balance of power and increase the risk of conflict.

Resource Nationalism and Economic Tensions

Baba Vanga warned of the rise of "resource nationalism," where nations assert control over their natural resources to prioritize domestic use or gain leverage in international negotiations. She foresaw countries limiting exports, imposing tariffs, or restricting access to key resources, particularly as they become more valuable. Her vision included scenarios where nations with rich energy resources wield their influence to gain political or economic concessions, creating tensions between resource-rich and resource-dependent countries.

Her prophecy suggests that while resource nationalism may benefit certain nations in the short term, it could ultimately lead to economic instability, trade disruptions, and strained diplomatic relationships. Baba Vanga's vision challenges countries to consider the long-term implications of resource nationalism and to explore cooperative strategies that promote shared prosperity.

Environmental and Ethical Concerns

Baba Vanga's prophecy also highlighted the environmental and ethical challenges associated with the pursuit of energy resources. She foresaw nations exploiting sensitive ecosystems and indigenous lands to access resources, leading to ecological degradation, loss of biodiversity, and displacement of local communities. Her vision included images of forests cleared for mining, rivers polluted by extraction processes, and communities struggling to protect their homes and heritage.

Her prophecy emphasizes the need for responsible resource management that balances economic interests with environmental stewardship and respect for human rights. Baba Vanga believed that without strict regulations and ethical considerations, the battle for energy resources could lead to irreversible damage, threatening the health of the planet and the well-being of future generations.

The Role of Technology and Innovation in Mitigating Conflict

While Baba Vanga's vision of energy wars was concerning, she also foresaw the potential for technology and innovation to offer solutions. She predicted advancements in energy efficiency, battery technology, and alternative energy sources that could reduce dependence on scarce resources. In her vision, new technologies such as nuclear fusion, hydrogen fuel cells, and enhanced battery storage create opportunities for nations to diversify their energy sources, reducing the likelihood of resource-driven conflict.

Her prophecy suggests that investing in technological research and development is critical for achieving energy security without exacerbating geopolitical tensions. Baba Vanga's vision challenges governments and the private sector to prioritize innovation and collaboration, working toward an energy landscape that is both sustainable and accessible.

The Need for International Cooperation

Baba Vanga's prophecy underscored the importance of international cooperation in managing energy resources. She foresaw a world where collaborative frameworks are essential for addressing energy-related conflicts, promoting resource-sharing agreements, and establishing policies for sustainable extraction and distribution. Her vision included initiatives such as energy alliances, global trade agreements, and technology-sharing programs designed to support equitable access to resources.

In her vision, Baba Vanga believed that countries must recognize their shared stake in energy security, approaching resource management as a collective responsibility rather than a competitive endeavor. She envisioned organizations like the United Nations playing a vital role in facilitating dialogue and creating guidelines for responsible resource use, helping to build trust and prevent conflicts.

The Role of Renewable Energy Partnerships

Baba Vanga foresaw that renewable energy partnerships would be a critical component of reducing resource competition and achieving energy security. She envisioned nations working together on large-scale renewable projects, such as cross-border solar grids, wind farms, and energy storage facilities, which could supply multiple regions and reduce dependence on any single resource.

This aspect of her prophecy aligns with contemporary initiatives to create transnational renewable energy networks, such as the African Clean Energy Corridor and the European Supergrid. Baba Vanga's vision suggests that by 2025, renewable energy partnerships could help countries diversify their energy sources, fostering collaboration and reducing the likelihood of energy-driven conflicts.

Lessons from Baba Vanga's Prophecy

Baba Vanga's predictions about energy wars and the battle for resources offer several key lessons for fostering a more cooperative and sustainable energy future:

- **Invest in Renewable Technologies:** Prioritizing renewable energy sources and developing alternative technologies can reduce dependency on limited resources.
- **Promote International Cooperation:** Collaborative frameworks and resource-sharing agreements can help mitigate energy-driven tensions and foster stability.
- **Address Resource Nationalism Carefully:** Balancing national interests with international responsibility is essential for maintaining global harmony.
- **Encourage Responsible Extraction:** Ensuring that resource management respects environmental and human rights is crucial for sustainable development.
- **Foster Innovation:** Advancing energy-efficient and alternative technologies can reduce competition for resources and create pathways for energy security.

Hope for a Sustainable Energy Future

Baba Vanga's vision of energy wars is ultimately a call for humanity to approach energy resource management with wisdom, responsibility, and shared purpose. While her prophecy highlights the risks of resource-driven conflicts, it also inspires hope for a future where technological innovation, international cooperation, and ethical stewardship guide humanity toward energy security.

As we continue to explore her predictions, Baba Vanga's insights challenge us to build a global energy landscape that promotes sustainability, equity, and peace. Her vision reminds us that the choices we make today about resource use and collaboration will shape the world of tomorrow, and that by working together, humanity can secure an energy future that benefits all.

Bioengineering and the Ethical Implications of 2025

Baba Vanga's predictions for 2025 included a vision of remarkable advances in bioengineering, highlighting the potential for breakthroughs in genetics, regenerative medicine, and synthetic biology. She foresaw a world where humanity has the tools to alter the genetic makeup of organisms, cure genetic diseases, and extend human capabilities. However, she also warned of profound ethical dilemmas and the risks associated with altering life's fundamental building blocks. This chapter delves into Baba Vanga's insights on bioengineering, exploring the promise of these technologies, their ethical challenges, and the importance of responsible application.

The Promise of Bioengineering

Baba Vanga envisioned a world where bioengineering transforms healthcare, agriculture, and even human potential. Her prophecy included:

- **Cures for Genetic Disorders:** Baba Vanga foresaw breakthroughs in gene therapy and gene editing, particularly with technologies like CRISPR, that would enable scientists to target and correct genetic mutations responsible for hereditary diseases. Her vision included the eradication of conditions like cystic fibrosis, sickle cell anemia, and muscular dystrophy, allowing individuals to lead healthier, longer lives.
- **Regenerative Medicine:** She predicted advancements in regenerative medicine, including tissue engineering and stem cell therapies, that would allow doctors to repair damaged organs, treat degenerative diseases, and even regenerate limbs. Her prophecy described a future where organ transplantation becomes less reliant on donors, thanks to lab-grown tissues and organs.
- **Synthetic Biology and Agriculture:** Baba Vanga foresaw the use of bioengineering in agriculture to address food security, including the development of crops that can withstand extreme climates, resist pests, and produce higher yields. In her vision, synthetic biology enables humanity to create more resilient and nutritious food sources, contributing to global food stability.

Her prophecy suggested that by 2025, bioengineering could profoundly impact both individuals and society, offering solutions to pressing health and environmental issues. Baba Vanga's vision was one of hope, emphasizing bioengineering's potential to alleviate suffering, increase sustainability, and unlock new possibilities for human well-being.

The Ethical Dilemmas of Genetic Modification

While optimistic, Baba Vanga also foresaw ethical dilemmas associated with genetic modification. She warned that the ability to alter DNA could lead to unintended consequences, particularly in the context of human enhancement. Her vision included the following ethical concerns:

- **"Designer" Traits and Inequality:** Baba Vanga warned of the potential for genetic engineering to be used beyond medical purposes, such as selecting for physical or intellectual traits. She foresaw a world where genetic modifications could create disparities, with those who can afford enhancements gaining advantages over others. Her prophecy emphasized the risk of "designer babies" and the ethical implications of choosing traits for offspring, suggesting that genetic modification could deepen social inequality.
- **Impact on Human Diversity:** Baba Vanga cautioned against using bioengineering to eliminate traits seen as undesirable, warning that this could reduce genetic diversity. Her vision included a plea to preserve the natural variations that define humanity, stressing that diversity is crucial to the resilience and adaptability of the human species.
- **Long-term Consequences:** Her prophecy also included concerns about the long-term impacts of genetic modifications on human evolution. Baba Vanga believed that altering DNA could have unforeseen effects on future generations, creating genetic changes that humanity may not fully understand or control.

Baba Vanga's prophecy challenges humanity to consider the ethical implications of genetic modification carefully, urging restraint and caution in choosing which applications of bioengineering are beneficial and which may carry unintended consequences.

Synthetic Biology and the Creation of Artificial Life

Baba Vanga foresaw advancements in synthetic biology that enable scientists to create artificial life forms. Her vision included organisms engineered to perform specific functions, such as cleaning polluted environments, producing biofuels, or synthesizing pharmaceuticals. While these applications offer promising benefits, she also warned of the ethical and ecological risks associated with creating artificial life.

Her prophecy included concerns about the potential release of synthetic organisms into natural ecosystems, where they could disrupt ecological balances. Baba Vanga emphasized the need for rigorous oversight and containment protocols, warning that even small alterations to the natural order could have widespread, irreversible consequences. Her vision suggests that humanity must approach synthetic biology with deep respect for the interconnectedness of life and a commitment to preventing harm.

Human Enhancement and the Ethics of "Improvement"

Baba Vanga also foresaw bioengineering leading to a future where humans could enhance their physical and cognitive abilities through genetic modifications or biotechnological implants. Her vision included potential enhancements like increased strength, resistance to disease, and even cognitive enhancements that boost intelligence or memory. However, she cautioned that such "improvements" could challenge our understanding of what it means to be human.

Her prophecy raised questions about identity, authenticity, and the potential for social division. Baba Vanga believed that while enhancing human abilities might offer individual benefits, it could also create ethical dilemmas, particularly if enhancements become a means of defining social status or success. Her vision suggests that humanity must consider whether altering human nature fundamentally respects or undermines the values of compassion, empathy, and interconnectedness.

The Importance of Regulation and Ethical Oversight

Baba Vanga's prophecy emphasized the role of regulation and ethical oversight in guiding bioengineering's development. She believed that without clear guidelines and accountability, bioengineering could lead to unintended harm, both for individuals and for society. Her vision called for international agreements and regulatory frameworks to ensure that bioengineering advances are aligned with humanity's highest ethical standards.

In her prophecy, Baba Vanga foresaw a need for collaboration among scientists, ethicists, and policymakers to establish protocols for responsible bioengineering. She believed that global cooperation is essential to prevent the misuse of these powerful technologies and to promote applications that benefit humanity as a whole. Baba Vanga's vision challenges leaders and researchers to prioritize ethics over expediency, ensuring that bioengineering remains a force for good.

Public Education and Awareness

Baba Vanga emphasized the importance of educating the public about bioengineering's potential and ethical implications. She foresaw a world where understanding the basics of genetic science and bioengineering is crucial for making informed decisions. Her prophecy included the idea that public awareness can empower individuals to engage in meaningful discussions about bioengineering, fostering a culture of transparency and accountability.

Her vision also stressed the need for ethical education, encouraging people to reflect on the implications of bioengineering beyond scientific possibilities. Baba Vanga believed that a well-informed public would help ensure that bioengineering advances align with shared values and collective well-being.

Balancing Innovation and Humanity

Baba Vanga's prophecy highlighted the importance of balancing innovation with respect for human dignity and natural diversity. She cautioned that while bioengineering offers profound opportunities, it must be guided by compassion, humility, and an appreciation for life's complexity. Her vision suggests that humanity should approach bioengineering with an attitude of stewardship, recognizing that the power to alter life also carries immense responsibility.

In her prophecy, Baba Vanga encouraged humanity to use bioengineering to enhance well-being without compromising the fundamental aspects of human nature and the natural world. Her vision is a call for balance, advocating for advancements that honor both individual aspirations and the collective integrity of humanity.

Lessons from Baba Vanga's Prophecy

Baba Vanga's insights on bioengineering and its ethical implications offer several key lessons for navigating this transformative field:

- **Promote Ethical Oversight:** Clear regulations and ethical frameworks are essential for ensuring that bioengineering serves the common good.
- **Preserve Human Diversity:** Maintaining genetic diversity and avoiding "designer" modifications can help safeguard the resilience and unity of humanity.

- **Educate and Empower the Public:** Public understanding of bioengineering fosters accountability and informed decision-making.
- **Balance Innovation with Ethics:** Using bioengineering to improve lives while respecting ethical principles can prevent misuse and protect human dignity.
- **Foster Global Cooperation:** International collaboration is vital to managing the global implications of bioengineering responsibly.

Hope for a Compassionate Future

Baba Vanga's vision of bioengineering is ultimately one of hope tempered with caution. While she foresaw bioengineering's potential to transform healthcare, agriculture, and human potential, she also emphasized the need for ethical responsibility and respect for life's inherent complexity. Her prophecy inspires humanity to approach bioengineering as a tool for healing, empowerment, and sustainability, while remaining mindful of the profound ethical questions it raises.

As we continue to explore her predictions, Baba Vanga's insights encourage us to guide bioengineering with a spirit of compassion, humility, and reverence for life. Her vision reminds us that in shaping the future of bioengineering, humanity has the opportunity to honor the delicate balance between progress and preservation, creating a world where innovation uplifts and unites all people.

The Future of Education According to Baba Vanga

Baba Vanga's predictions for 2025 included a vision of profound changes in education, driven by advances in technology and a shift in societal values. She foresaw a future where education evolves beyond traditional classrooms to embrace personalized, accessible, and globally connected learning experiences. Her prophecy suggested that by reimagining how people learn and teach, humanity could cultivate a generation equipped not only with knowledge but also with critical thinking, empathy, and adaptability. In this chapter, we explore Baba Vanga's vision for the future of education, examining new learning models, technological innovations, and the ethical challenges of redefined educational systems.

The Transformation of Traditional Classrooms

Baba Vanga foresaw that the traditional classroom structure would be transformed by 2025, giving way to more flexible and student-centered learning environments. Her vision included a shift from rote memorization and standardized testing toward active, personalized, and experiential learning. She predicted that schools and educational institutions would adopt more dynamic approaches, encouraging curiosity, collaboration, and real-world problem-solving.

In her prophecy, she described classrooms that incorporate interactive learning stations, virtual simulations, and project-based tasks. Baba Vanga believed that by allowing students to explore topics in depth and apply knowledge creatively, education would foster independent thinkers and lifelong learners who are well-prepared for the complexities of the modern world.

Personalized Learning and Adaptive Education Technologies

Baba Vanga envisioned the rise of personalized learning, where education is tailored to each student's unique strengths, weaknesses, and learning pace. She foresaw advancements in adaptive education technologies—powered by artificial intelligence—that would assess students' progress in real-time and adjust lessons accordingly. Her vision included AI-driven tutoring systems that provide individual support, helping students grasp challenging concepts and build confidence in their abilities.

Her prophecy suggested that by 2025, education would shift from a one-size-fits-all model to a personalized approach, enabling students to pursue subjects at their own pace and in ways that resonate with them. Baba Vanga believed that personalized learning would help students overcome learning barriers, foster their interests, and encourage a deeper understanding of their studies.

Global Access to Education

Baba Vanga predicted a future where education is accessible to everyone, regardless of geographic location or economic status. She foresaw the rise of digital platforms and virtual classrooms, making high-quality education available to students in remote or underserved regions. In her vision, mobile devices, internet access, and open-source educational content bridge gaps, allowing students around the world to learn from the same resources as their urban counterparts.

This aspect of her prophecy aligns with current efforts to increase digital literacy and access in developing regions. Baba Vanga's vision suggests that by embracing technology and inclusive policies, education can become a universal right, empowering people worldwide with the knowledge and skills needed to pursue their goals.

Collaborative and Peer-Led Learning Models

Baba Vanga foresaw a shift toward collaborative and peer-led learning models, where students learn from one another as much as they do from teachers. Her vision included virtual and in-person communities where students from diverse backgrounds and locations come together to share insights, work on projects, and solve real-world problems collectively. She believed that this peer-to-peer approach would enhance creativity, empathy, and teamwork.

In her prophecy, Baba Vanga emphasized that learning in a collaborative environment would teach students to value multiple perspectives and develop interpersonal skills. Her vision suggested that this shift could prepare students to thrive in a globally connected world, where working across cultural and disciplinary boundaries is increasingly common.

Focus on Critical Thinking and Emotional Intelligence

Baba Vanga's vision of the future of education placed a strong emphasis on critical thinking, creativity, and emotional intelligence as core components of the curriculum. She foresaw a world where students are encouraged to question, analyze, and solve complex problems, rather than simply memorizing facts. Her prophecy included the development of courses that teach students how to think independently, make ethical decisions, and manage their emotions effectively.

In her vision, emotional intelligence and mental well-being are prioritized alongside academic knowledge, with students learning skills in empathy, resilience, and conflict resolution. Baba Vanga believed that education should nurture the whole person, equipping students with the emotional and cognitive tools needed to navigate life's challenges with wisdom and compassion.

Virtual and Augmented Reality in Education

Baba Vanga foresaw virtual and augmented reality playing a significant role in the future of education. She predicted that immersive learning experiences would allow students to explore historical events, scientific phenomena, and global cultures in engaging, hands-on ways. Her vision included virtual reality (VR) simulations that transport students to different time periods, distant ecosystems, and complex mathematical models, offering a learning experience that feels both real and interactive.

Her prophecy suggested that by 2025, these immersive technologies would make abstract concepts more tangible, enhancing students' understanding and retention. Baba Vanga believed that virtual and augmented reality could make learning more engaging, helping students connect with subjects they might otherwise find challenging or inaccessible.

The Role of Ethics and Digital Literacy

While optimistic about the impact of technology on education, Baba Vanga also foresaw the need for ethics and digital literacy as central components of the curriculum. She warned of the risks associated with digital misinformation, online privacy concerns, and over-reliance on technology. Her vision included courses on digital citizenship, critical media analysis, and responsible internet use, equipping students with the skills to navigate an increasingly digital world responsibly.

Her prophecy emphasized the importance of helping students understand both the benefits and pitfalls of technology. Baba Vanga believed that by fostering digital literacy and ethical awareness, education could prepare students to use technology responsibly, making informed choices that benefit themselves and society.

The Evolving Role of Educators

Baba Vanga foresaw a transformation in the role of educators, seeing teachers as facilitators of learning rather than mere transmitters of information. Her vision included teachers who guide students in critical thinking, support individualized learning, and encourage exploration. She believed that educators would play a more collaborative role, working alongside AI-driven tools to create enriching learning experiences.

In her prophecy, Baba Vanga highlighted the importance of educators fostering meaningful connections with students, serving as mentors who support emotional growth and inspire intellectual curiosity. Her vision challenges educational systems to support teachers with training and resources, empowering them to thrive in this evolving role and to continue being an essential part of the learning experience.

Lifelong Learning and Skill Development

Baba Vanga's vision of education extended beyond traditional schooling, emphasizing the importance of lifelong learning. She foresaw a future where individuals regularly update their skills, adapting to changing career landscapes and personal interests. Her prophecy included a world where education becomes a continuous journey, with people taking online courses, attending workshops, and engaging in self-directed learning throughout their lives.

In her vision, this culture of lifelong learning enables people to remain adaptable, resilient, and open to new opportunities. Baba Vanga believed that lifelong learning would be essential for individuals and societies to thrive in an era of rapid change, fostering personal fulfillment and collective growth.

Lessons from Baba Vanga's Prophecy

Baba Vanga's predictions about the future of education offer several key lessons for creating a more inclusive and effective educational system:

- **Prioritize Personalization:** Adapting education to individual learning needs can foster deeper understanding and engagement.
- **Embrace Global Access:** Making education accessible to all, regardless of location or economic status, is essential for empowering future generations.
- **Promote Collaborative Learning:** Encouraging students to work together and learn from diverse perspectives can foster empathy and creativity.
- **Integrate Emotional Intelligence:** Focusing on emotional intelligence and critical thinking prepares students for personal and professional success.
- **Educate for Digital Literacy:** Preparing students to navigate a digital world responsibly can protect them from misinformation and foster ethical technology use.

Hope for an Enlightened Future

Baba Vanga's vision of education is ultimately one of hope and possibility. She believed that by transforming education, humanity could nurture individuals who are not only knowledgeable but also compassionate, innovative, and resilient. Her prophecy suggests that education has the power to shape the future by equipping people with the skills, values, and understanding needed to create a better world.

As we continue to explore her predictions, Baba Vanga's insights challenge us to rethink how we approach learning and teaching. Her vision inspires us to create educational systems that honor each person's potential, cultivate curiosity, and promote a culture of lifelong growth. By embracing her vision, humanity can move toward a future where education uplifts all people, empowering them to lead lives of purpose and meaning.

Global Unification or Fragmentation? Baba Vanga's Vision

Baba Vanga's predictions for 2025 included a vision of humanity at a crossroads, facing a pivotal choice between global unification and fragmentation. She foresaw a world where nations either come together to address shared challenges or become increasingly divided by cultural, political, and economic differences. Her prophecy suggested that the outcome would depend on humanity's willingness to prioritize collective well-being over individual interests. In this chapter, we explore Baba Vanga's vision of global unification versus fragmentation, examining the factors that could lead down each path and the implications for the future of humanity.

The Push toward Global Unification

Baba Vanga envisioned the possibility of a unified world, where nations set aside differences and collaborate to address issues like climate change, resource scarcity, and public health. She believed that this unification would be driven by a growing awareness of shared human experiences and interdependence. Her vision included:

- **Collective Action on Global Issues:** Baba Vanga foresaw countries working together on a scale never seen before, forming alliances to tackle pressing global challenges. She predicted cooperative efforts in areas such as environmental conservation, food security, disease prevention, and poverty alleviation. Her vision included global summits, international treaties, and resource-sharing agreements designed to foster mutual support and a sense of shared responsibility.
- **Technological and Scientific Collaboration:** In her prophecy, Baba Vanga saw a world where technological and scientific advancements transcend national borders, enabling countries to pool resources and knowledge. She believed that breakthroughs in medicine, renewable energy, and space exploration could be achieved more rapidly through collaborative research, with nations working together toward common goals.
- **Cultural Exchange and Mutual Understanding:** Baba Vanga's vision of unification extended beyond politics and economics. She foresaw a world where cultural exchange and mutual understanding bridge divides, fostering empathy and appreciation for diversity. Her vision included educational programs, media collaborations, and virtual platforms that connect people from different backgrounds, encouraging dialogue and respect.

Baba Vanga believed that global unification would create a more stable, prosperous, and peaceful world, where humanity is guided by compassion, cooperation, and shared purpose. Her prophecy emphasized that unification requires countries to recognize the benefits of interdependence and to approach international relations with humility and openness.

The Risk of Fragmentation and Division

While Baba Vanga saw hope in unification, she also foresaw a scenario where the world becomes increasingly fragmented, divided by political, cultural, and economic conflicts. Her vision of fragmentation included:

- **Nationalism and Protectionism:** Baba Vanga predicted that rising nationalism and protectionist policies could drive nations to prioritize their own interests over global collaboration. Her vision included countries implementing strict border controls, restricting trade, and competing for resources. This inward focus, she believed, would lead to isolation and heighten tensions between nations, as each pursues its own agenda without regard for global consequences.

- **Cultural and Ideological Conflicts:** Baba Vanga foresaw cultural and ideological differences leading to conflicts, as societies struggle to reconcile divergent values and beliefs. She warned that misunderstandings and stereotypes could lead to mistrust and hostility, driving a wedge between communities. Her prophecy suggested that without efforts to foster mutual respect, humanity could face divisions that erode the fabric of global unity.
- **Economic Disparities and Resource Competition:** In her vision, economic inequality and competition for scarce resources could drive nations apart. Baba Vanga foresaw wealthier nations hoarding resources and using their economic power to influence global decisions, creating resentment and exacerbating inequality. She believed that this competition for resources could lead to a breakdown of trust, as countries prioritize self-preservation over equitable solutions.

Baba Vanga's vision of fragmentation serves as a cautionary tale, warning that the pursuit of individual or national interests without regard for the common good could lead to instability, conflict, and a less resilient world.

The Role of International Organizations and Alliances

Baba Vanga saw international organizations playing a central role in either fostering unification or exacerbating fragmentation. She foresaw organizations like the United Nations, World Health Organization, and regional alliances taking on greater responsibility in promoting peace, security, and cooperation. Her vision included international bodies serving as platforms for dialogue, dispute resolution, and the implementation of global agreements.

However, she also warned that these organizations could become sources of division if they are perceived as biased or ineffective. Baba Vanga's prophecy suggests that the success of international organizations depends on their ability to operate transparently, represent diverse voices, and address issues equitably. She believed that inclusive and accountable organizations could help guide humanity toward unification, while weakened or divisive institutions could contribute to fragmentation.

Technological Influence on Global Unity

Baba Vanga predicted that technology would play a crucial role in shaping the future of global unity. She foresaw digital platforms, social media, and virtual communication tools creating opportunities for people to connect across borders, fostering a sense of global community. Her vision included the use of technology to facilitate real-time information sharing, collaborative problem-solving, and grassroots movements that unite people around shared causes.

However, she also warned of technology's potential to fuel fragmentation if it becomes a tool for disinformation, surveillance, or polarization. Baba Vanga's prophecy highlighted the importance of digital literacy, ethical media practices, and policies that promote open, respectful dialogue. She believed that technology could either bridge divides or deepen them, depending on how it is developed, regulated, and used.

Education as a Force for Unity

Baba Vanga saw education as a powerful tool for fostering global unity. She foresaw schools and universities embracing curricula that emphasize global awareness, cultural sensitivity, and ethical responsibility. Her vision included programs that teach students about different cultures, languages, and perspectives, preparing them to engage with people from diverse backgrounds.

Her prophecy also included an emphasis on teaching critical thinking and empathy, helping students understand and respect multiple viewpoints. Baba Vanga believed that education could create a generation of leaders who prioritize cooperation and inclusivity, promoting unity in an increasingly interconnected world.

Ethical Leadership and the Path Forward

Baba Vanga's prophecy underscored the importance of ethical leadership in guiding humanity toward unification. She foresaw the rise of leaders who value transparency, compassion, and a commitment to the common good. Her vision included leaders who prioritize dialogue over conflict, advocate for fair and inclusive policies, and inspire people to look beyond national or cultural divisions.

In her vision, Baba Vanga emphasized that ethical leadership is essential for building trust between nations and communities. She believed that leaders who embody integrity and empathy can help humanity overcome divisions, fostering a sense of shared purpose and unity.

The Choice between Unity and Division

Baba Vanga's prophecy presents humanity with a choice between unity and division. She believed that while fragmentation may seem easier in times of uncertainty, unification offers the potential for lasting peace and progress. Her vision challenged nations to recognize their interconnectedness and to approach international relations with humility, compassion, and a focus on common goals.

Her prophecy suggests that the future of humanity hinges on its collective willingness to address challenges together, acknowledging that only through unity can humanity achieve sustainable prosperity and resilience.

Lessons from Baba Vanga's Prophecy

Baba Vanga's predictions about global unification or fragmentation offer several key lessons for guiding humanity toward a harmonious future:

- **Promote Inclusive Collaboration:** Emphasizing mutual support and shared goals can help build trust and cooperation between nations.
- **Address Economic Inequality:** Ensuring equitable access to resources and opportunities can reduce tensions and foster unity.
- **Foster Ethical Leadership:** Leaders who prioritize the common good, empathy, and transparency can inspire cooperation and strengthen global bonds.
- **Educate for Global Awareness:** Teaching respect for diversity and fostering cultural understanding can create a foundation for peace and unity.
- **Use Technology Responsibly:** Ensuring that technology is used to connect rather than divide can support efforts toward global unification.

Hope for a Unified World

Baba Vanga's vision of unification offers a hopeful path for humanity, one where nations come together to build a world based on compassion, collaboration, and shared responsibility. Her prophecy suggests that while the road to unification may be challenging, it holds the promise of a future where humanity transcends its differences to work toward common goals.

As we conclude her predictions, Baba Vanga's insights remind us of the power of unity in addressing the complexities of a rapidly changing world. Her vision challenges humanity to choose collaboration over conflict, empathy over isolation, and shared purpose over division. By embracing her vision of global unification, we can create a world where all people have the opportunity to thrive, finding strength and resilience in our interconnectedness.

Prophecies on the Changing Role of Women in Society

Baba Vanga's predictions for 2025 included a vision of profound transformations in the role of women in society. She foresaw a world where women gain unprecedented levels of influence, breaking free from historical limitations to become powerful leaders, innovators, and agents of social change. Her prophecy suggested that as women step into roles of greater responsibility, they bring unique perspectives and values that positively impact governance, industry, and community life. This chapter explores Baba Vanga's vision for the evolving role of women, examining the factors driving this transformation and the implications for society at large.

The Rise of Women in Leadership

Baba Vanga foresaw a significant rise in women holding leadership positions across all sectors, including politics, business, science, and education. Her vision included a future where women are no longer underrepresented in positions of power but are instead respected and influential leaders shaping policies and innovations. She predicted that female leaders would bring a collaborative and empathetic approach to governance, prioritizing social welfare, sustainability, and long-term vision.

In her prophecy, Baba Vanga emphasized that women's leadership would help address global challenges, from climate change to economic inequality. She believed that by bringing their unique insights and values to the table, women could create more inclusive and resilient systems that reflect the needs of all people. Baba Vanga's vision suggests that by 2025, the world may witness a new era of governance and leadership, where women's contributions are valued as essential to global progress.

Women as Innovators and Change-Makers

Baba Vanga predicted that women would increasingly become prominent innovators and change-makers, particularly in fields like science, technology, and social entrepreneurship. She foresaw a world where women lead groundbreaking research, drive technological advancements, and launch initiatives that uplift communities. Her vision included women taking on influential roles in healthcare, renewable energy, education, and artificial intelligence, using their knowledge and creativity to improve quality of life and create sustainable solutions.

In her prophecy, Baba Vanga highlighted the importance of providing women with equal opportunities to access education and resources. She believed that as barriers to women's participation in traditionally male-dominated fields are dismantled, society will benefit from a more diverse pool of talent and ideas. Baba Vanga's vision encourages a future where women's potential is fully realized, bringing fresh perspectives and innovations that address the world's most pressing issues.

Women's Role in Shaping Ethical and Inclusive Policies

Baba Vanga's vision of the future included women playing a central role in shaping ethical and inclusive policies. She foresaw women leaders advocating for human rights, gender equality, and social justice, challenging systems that perpetuate discrimination or inequality. Her prophecy suggested that as more women enter positions of influence, they would prioritize policies that reflect compassion, fairness, and inclusivity, creating societies where everyone is valued and protected.

Her vision also included women's advocacy for work-life balance, family support systems, and mental health resources, recognizing that these elements are essential for a healthy and thriving society. Baba Vanga believed that women's approach to policymaking would create a more humane and equitable world, ensuring that economic progress is balanced with social well-being. Her prophecy suggests that women's voices in policymaking will be instrumental in advancing fairness and empathy within social structures.

The Transformation of Gender Roles and Family Dynamics

Baba Vanga foresaw a transformation in traditional gender roles, with society embracing more flexible and inclusive definitions of family, work, and personal fulfillment. She predicted that both women and men would have greater freedom to pursue careers, raise families, and contribute to society in ways that reflect their individual strengths and interests, rather than being constrained by outdated expectations.

Her prophecy included a shift toward shared responsibilities in parenting and household duties, with both partners playing active roles in family life. Baba Vanga believed that this evolution would benefit children and communities, as families adapt to values of equality and cooperation. She envisioned a future where individuals feel empowered to pursue fulfilling lives that balance personal and professional aspirations, promoting a society where each person's contributions are equally valued.

Increased Focus on Women's Health and Well-Being

Baba Vanga predicted that the changing role of women in society would lead to increased attention on women's health and well-being. She foresaw advancements in reproductive health, mental health services, and women-specific healthcare research, addressing issues that have historically been overlooked. Her vision included improvements in maternal care, access to mental health resources, and support for women experiencing gender-based violence.

Her prophecy emphasized that as society recognizes the importance of women's well-being, more resources would be allocated to support women's physical and emotional health. Baba Vanga believed that addressing these aspects of well-being is essential not only for individual women but also for creating strong, resilient communities. Her vision challenges society to prioritize women's health as a foundational aspect of social progress.

Education as a Key to Empowerment

Baba Vanga foresaw education playing a crucial role in empowering women to reach their full potential. She predicted that as more women gain access to quality education, they will be better equipped to pursue careers, lead initiatives, and contribute to social and economic growth. Her vision included an emphasis on STEM (science, technology, engineering, and mathematics) education, leadership training, and vocational programs that provide women with the skills and confidence needed to succeed in diverse fields.

In her prophecy, Baba Vanga also highlighted the importance of education that emphasizes critical thinking, ethical decision-making, and social responsibility. She believed that educated women would inspire positive change in their communities, serving as role models and advocates for progress. Baba Vanga's vision suggests that by investing in women's education, society can unlock new possibilities for innovation, leadership, and social harmony.

The Role of Female Mentorship and Solidarity

Baba Vanga foresaw the importance of female mentorship and solidarity in helping women achieve their goals. She envisioned networks of women supporting each other, sharing knowledge, and advocating for equal opportunities. Her prophecy included a world where women's mentorship programs, professional organizations, and grassroots movements create a sense of unity and empowerment among women.

In her vision, Baba Vanga believed that female solidarity would play a vital role in breaking down barriers and addressing systemic challenges. She saw women's mentorship as a source of inspiration and guidance, helping women overcome obstacles and reach their potential. Her prophecy encourages women to support each other's growth, fostering a culture of collaboration and collective empowerment.

Challenges and the Path Forward

While Baba Vanga's vision was hopeful, she also foresaw challenges that would require persistence and dedication. She recognized that dismantling centuries-old biases and structures would not be easy and that women may face resistance in their journey toward equality. Her prophecy included a call for resilience, urging women and their allies to continue advocating for progress despite obstacles.

Baba Vanga also warned of the risk of superficial change, where token representation or symbolic gestures replace meaningful action. Her vision emphasized the need for genuine transformation, where societal values and institutions reflect a true commitment to equality. Baba Vanga believed that the path forward requires both men and women to work together, embracing values of respect, equity, and justice.

Lessons from Baba Vanga's Prophecy

Baba Vanga's predictions about the changing role of women in society offer several key lessons for fostering a more inclusive and equitable world:

- **Support Women in Leadership:** Creating pathways for women to hold positions of power and influence can drive positive change across sectors.
- **Promote Equal Opportunity in Education:** Providing quality education and resources empowers women to pursue diverse careers and contribute to social progress.
- **Prioritize Women's Health and Well-Being:** Addressing women's physical and mental health needs is essential for building resilient communities.
- **Foster Flexible Family Dynamics:** Embracing inclusive family structures and shared responsibilities can support both personal and professional growth.
- **Encourage Female Solidarity:** Mentorship and support networks empower women to reach their potential and inspire others to do the same.

Hope for an Inclusive Future

Baba Vanga's vision of the changing role of women in society is one of optimism and transformation. She believed that as women step into roles of leadership, innovation, and advocacy, they bring values of compassion, resilience, and inclusivity that benefit all of society. Her prophecy suggests that by embracing women's contributions, humanity can create a more balanced and harmonious world.

As we continue to explore her predictions, Baba Vanga's insights challenge us to support women's empowerment and to recognize the power of diversity in shaping a brighter future. Her vision reminds us that true progress lies in honoring the potential of every individual, fostering a society where all people have the opportunity to lead, create, and thrive together.

The Balance of Nature: Ecological Harmony or Destruction?

Baba Vanga's predictions for 2025 emphasized the critical relationship between humanity and the natural world, presenting a stark choice: either restore ecological harmony or face the devastating consequences of environmental destruction. She foresaw a world at a tipping point, where the actions of individuals, communities, and governments determine whether the planet thrives or suffers irreversible damage. In this chapter, we explore Baba Vanga's vision of humanity's impact on nature, the consequences of ecological imbalance, and the pathways toward a harmonious coexistence with the environment.

The Fragile State of the Planet

Baba Vanga foresaw that by 2025, the planet's ecosystems would be under immense strain due to deforestation, pollution, and climate change. She envisioned the rapid loss of biodiversity, with many species pushed to the brink of extinction as habitats are destroyed and ecosystems disrupted. Her vision included images of oceans polluted with plastic, air filled with smog, and forests reduced to barren landscapes.

Her prophecy warned that these environmental pressures would not only affect wildlife but also have cascading effects on humanity, including food shortages, water scarcity, and increased vulnerability to natural disasters. Baba Vanga's vision challenges humanity to recognize the interconnectedness of all life and to take immediate action to protect and restore the natural world.

The Consequences of Ecological Destruction

Baba Vanga's vision highlighted the devastating consequences of failing to address ecological degradation. She foresaw:

- **Intensified Natural Disasters:** Baba Vanga predicted that climate change would lead to more frequent and severe natural disasters, including hurricanes, floods, droughts, and wildfires. These events, she believed, would disrupt communities, strain resources, and exacerbate global inequalities.
- **Food and Water Insecurity:** Her prophecy included warnings about the depletion of fertile soil, overfishing of oceans, and pollution of freshwater sources. She believed that without sustainable practices, humanity could face widespread food and water shortages, threatening the stability of societies around the world.
- **Loss of Biodiversity:** Baba Vanga foresaw a world where ecosystems collapse due to the extinction of key species. She warned that the loss of biodiversity would disrupt the delicate balance of nature, reducing the planet's ability to sustain life and recover from environmental shocks.

Her vision emphasizes the urgency of addressing these issues, suggesting that ecological destruction could have far-reaching and irreversible effects on the health and prosperity of future generations.

The Path toward Ecological Harmony

While Baba Vanga's prophecy included warnings, she also envisioned a hopeful path toward ecological harmony. She foresaw humanity embracing sustainable practices, prioritizing conservation, and adopting technologies that protect and restore the environment. Her vision included:

- **Renewable Energy Transition:** Baba Vanga predicted a shift away from fossil fuels toward renewable energy sources like solar, wind, and geothermal power. She believed that this transition would reduce greenhouse gas emissions, slow the pace of climate change, and promote energy independence.

- **Reforestation and Habitat Restoration:** Her prophecy included large-scale efforts to restore forests, wetlands, and other critical ecosystems. Baba Vanga foresaw communities planting trees, protecting endangered species, and rehabilitating degraded lands to create habitats that support biodiversity and resilience.
- **Sustainable Agriculture and Fishing:** Baba Vanga envisioned a future where agriculture and fishing practices align with environmental sustainability. She foresaw innovations such as precision farming, permaculture, and aquaculture reducing the environmental impact of food production while ensuring food security for a growing population.

Her vision suggests that by embracing these strategies, humanity can repair the damage done to the planet and create a future where people and nature coexist in harmony.

The Role of Technology in Environmental Restoration

Baba Vanga foresaw technology playing a crucial role in restoring ecological balance. She predicted advancements in environmental monitoring, renewable energy, and pollution control that would enable humanity to better understand and address environmental challenges. Her vision included:

- **Climate Modeling and Prediction:** Baba Vanga envisioned the use of AI and big data to model climate patterns, predict natural disasters, and inform sustainable development strategies.
- **Pollution Cleanup Technologies:** Her prophecy included innovations such as biodegradable materials, waste recycling systems, and technologies that remove pollutants from air, water, and soil.
- **Carbon Capture and Storage:** Baba Vanga foresaw technologies that capture and store carbon dioxide, helping to mitigate the impacts of industrial emissions and reduce atmospheric greenhouse gas levels.

Her vision emphasizes that while technology is a powerful tool, its effectiveness depends on humanity's commitment to using it responsibly and ethically to benefit the environment.

The Importance of Education and Advocacy

Baba Vanga believed that education and advocacy are essential for fostering a culture of environmental stewardship. She foresaw schools incorporating environmental science and ethics into their curricula, teaching students about the importance of conservation, sustainable living, and the interconnectedness of ecosystems. Her vision included grassroots movements, community initiatives, and global campaigns that inspire individuals to take action.

In her prophecy, Baba Vanga highlighted the power of collective effort, suggesting that when individuals work together to protect the environment, they can create meaningful change. She believed that public awareness and engagement are key to building momentum for policies and practices that promote ecological harmony.

The Role of Ethical Leadership

Baba Vanga foresaw the emergence of leaders who prioritize environmental protection and sustainability in their policies. She believed that ethical leadership is essential for addressing ecological challenges and guiding humanity toward a more harmonious relationship with nature. Her vision included leaders advocating for renewable energy investments, conservation programs, and international agreements to combat climate change.

Her prophecy emphasized that effective leadership must be transparent, inclusive, and rooted in a long-term vision. Baba Vanga believed that leaders who embody these qualities can inspire trust and mobilize societies to work together for the common good.

The Need for Global Cooperation

Baba Vanga's vision of ecological harmony relied heavily on global cooperation. She foresaw nations coming together to share knowledge, resources, and technologies to address environmental challenges. Her prophecy included international agreements to reduce carbon emissions, protect biodiversity, and regulate industries that impact the environment.

In her vision, Baba Vanga emphasized that no single nation can solve global ecological issues alone. She believed that collaboration and solidarity are essential for creating a sustainable future, where all countries contribute to and benefit from environmental protection efforts.

Lessons from Baba Vanga's Prophecy

Baba Vanga's predictions about the balance of nature offer several key lessons for fostering ecological harmony:

- **Adopt Sustainable Practices:** Embracing renewable energy, sustainable agriculture, and conservation initiatives is essential for protecting the planet.
- **Leverage Technology Responsibly:** Using innovative technologies to monitor, restore, and protect ecosystems can accelerate progress toward sustainability.
- **Educate and Engage the Public:** Raising awareness and fostering a sense of responsibility among individuals and communities can drive meaningful environmental action.
- **Promote Ethical Leadership:** Leaders who prioritize sustainability and transparency can inspire trust and mobilize societies to act collectively.
- **Strengthen Global Cooperation:** Collaborative efforts between nations are critical for addressing shared environmental challenges and achieving long-term balance.

Hope for a Sustainable Future

Baba Vanga's vision of ecological harmony reflects her belief in humanity's capacity to adapt and thrive in balance with nature. While her prophecy highlights the risks of ecological destruction, it also inspires hope for a future where people and the planet coexist harmoniously. She believed that by embracing responsibility, innovation, and collaboration, humanity can create a world where nature flourishes, and all life benefits from its abundance.

As we conclude her predictions, Baba Vanga's insights remind us that the choices we make today will shape the planet for generations to come. Her vision challenges us to honor our connection to the natural world, fostering a culture of care, respect, and sustainability that ensures a thriving Earth for all.

Baba Vanga on the Role of Media and Truth in 2025

Baba Vanga's predictions for 2025 included profound insights into the evolving role of media and its influence on society's perception of truth. She foresaw a world where the rapid dissemination of information could either unite people through shared understanding or divide them through misinformation and manipulation. Her prophecy suggested that the media would become a powerful force for shaping public opinion, demanding greater accountability, ethical standards, and public vigilance. This chapter explores Baba Vanga's vision for the role of media and truth in 2025, examining the challenges, responsibilities, and opportunities for media to uphold its integrity in a complex, interconnected world.

The Power of Media in Shaping Society

Baba Vanga predicted that by 2025, media would hold unparalleled power in shaping societal beliefs, behaviors, and decisions. She foresaw media as a double-edged sword: a tool capable of promoting understanding, education, and positive change, but also vulnerable to misuse for spreading propaganda, misinformation, and division. In her vision, media platforms wield influence over politics, culture, and personal perceptions, making them central to the way individuals interact with the world.

Her prophecy emphasized the importance of recognizing this power and ensuring that media is used responsibly. Baba Vanga believed that ethical journalism and transparency would be critical for fostering trust and maintaining societal cohesion.

The Rise of Digital Media and Its Impacts

Baba Vanga foresaw the continued dominance of digital media, with social platforms, news websites, and streaming services becoming primary sources of information. She predicted that this shift would democratize information, allowing people to access diverse viewpoints and engage in global conversations. However, she also warned of challenges arising from the speed and volume of digital content:

Misinformation and Disinformation: Baba Vanga foresaw a rise in the spread of false information, fueled by the ease of sharing unverified content online. She believed that misinformation could erode trust in institutions, deepen divisions, and create confusion about critical issues.

Echo Chambers and Polarization: Her prophecy included concerns about people gravitating toward media that reinforces their existing beliefs, leading to echo chambers that isolate individuals from differing perspectives. Baba Vanga warned that this polarization could hinder dialogue, compromise critical thinking, and exacerbate societal divides.

Loss of Credibility: Baba Vanga foresaw that the abundance of unreliable sources would challenge traditional media outlets to maintain their credibility. She believed that trust in media would become fragile, with audiences increasingly skeptical of the information they consume.

Her vision suggests that while digital media offers unparalleled access to knowledge, its unregulated nature requires vigilance and discernment from both creators and consumers.

Media Ethics and the Responsibility of Truth

Baba Vanga emphasized the ethical responsibilities of media creators, predicting that their actions would significantly influence societal well-being. She foresaw a world where media outlets and platforms are held to higher standards of accuracy, fairness, and transparency. Her vision included:

- **Fact-Checking and Accountability:** Baba Vanga believed that rigorous fact-checking and accountability are essential for maintaining trust in media. She foresaw organizations implementing stricter editorial policies, employing advanced tools for verifying information, and making corrections promptly and visibly.
- **Balanced Reporting:** Her prophecy highlighted the importance of balanced reporting that presents multiple perspectives, helping audiences form informed opinions. Baba Vanga believed that responsible media should resist sensationalism and prioritize stories that contribute to public understanding and progress.
- **Protection from Influence:** Baba Vanga foresaw the need for media to maintain independence from political and corporate pressures. She believed that ensuring editorial freedom is essential for preserving the integrity of journalism and its role as a watchdog for democracy.

Her vision challenges media creators to act with integrity, recognizing their role in shaping perceptions and fostering informed, cohesive societies.

The Role of Technology in Media and Truth

Baba Vanga foresaw technology playing a dual role in the media landscape, offering tools to enhance accuracy and reach while also enabling the spread of false narratives. Her prophecy included:

AI and Automation in Journalism: Baba Vanga predicted that artificial intelligence would streamline reporting, assisting with data analysis, content creation, and fact-checking. She believed that AI could enhance efficiency and accuracy if used responsibly.

Detection of Misinformation: Her vision included advancements in technology to identify and flag false information. Baba Vanga foresaw algorithms and blockchain systems being developed to verify the authenticity of news and protect audiences from manipulation.

Potential for Deepfakes and Manipulation: Baba Vanga warned of the risks posed by technologies like deepfakes, which could distort reality and deceive audiences. She emphasized the need for tools and policies to detect and counteract such manipulations.

Her prophecy suggests that while technology offers solutions for improving media integrity, it also requires careful management to prevent misuse and ensure trustworthiness.

Media Literacy and Public Awareness

Baba Vanga believed that fostering media literacy is essential for navigating the complexities of the modern media landscape. She foresaw education systems incorporating courses on critical thinking, fact-checking, and ethical media consumption. Her vision included:

- **Empowering Audiences:** Baba Vanga foresaw individuals becoming more discerning consumers of media, questioning sources, verifying information, and seeking diverse viewpoints. She believed that an informed public is less susceptible to manipulation and better equipped to engage in meaningful dialogue.
- **Promoting Ethical Engagement:** Her prophecy included campaigns and initiatives to promote respectful

online behavior and combat misinformation. Baba Vanga believed that fostering a culture of digital citizenship would help mitigate the negative effects of online discourse.

Her vision highlights the importance of equipping individuals with the tools to navigate media responsibly, fostering a society where truth and understanding prevail.

The Role of Media in Bridging Divides

Baba Vanga foresaw media playing a critical role in bridging societal divides and fostering global understanding. She predicted that media could highlight shared human experiences, promote empathy, and encourage collaboration on global challenges. Her vision included:

- **Storytelling as a Unifier:** Baba Vanga believed that storytelling has the power to connect people across cultures, providing a platform for marginalized voices and diverse perspectives. She foresaw media amplifying stories that inspire compassion and solidarity.
- **Promoting Dialogue:** Her prophecy included the use of media as a platform for constructive dialogue, where differing opinions can be shared and debated respectfully. Baba Vanga believed that fostering open communication is essential for resolving conflicts and building trust.

Her vision suggests that when media prioritizes unity and understanding, it can become a powerful force for social cohesion and progress.

Lessons from Baba Vanga's Prophecy

Baba Vanga's insights on the role of media and truth in 2025 offer several key lessons for navigating the evolving media landscape:

- **Uphold Media Ethics:** Ensuring accuracy, transparency, and fairness in reporting is essential for maintaining public trust.
- **Foster Media Literacy:** Educating individuals to critically evaluate media content can empower them to make informed decisions.
- **Leverage Technology Responsibly:** Using AI and other tools to enhance media integrity can counteract the spread of misinformation.
- **Promote Balanced Narratives:** Amplifying diverse perspectives and prioritizing constructive dialogue can help bridge societal divides.
- **Encourage Accountability:** Holding media creators and platforms responsible for their content ensures that truth remains a guiding principle.

Hope for a Truthful Media Landscape

Baba Vanga's vision of media and truth reflects her belief in the power of information to shape the world for better or worse. While her prophecy highlights the challenges of misinformation and manipulation, it also inspires hope for a future where media serves as a force for unity, education, and progress. She believed that by prioritizing ethics, fostering media literacy, and leveraging technology responsibly, humanity can create a media landscape that upholds truth and empowers people to thrive.

As we conclude this chapter, Baba Vanga's insights remind us of the immense responsibility that media carries and the collective effort required to ensure its integrity. Her vision challenges us to approach media with discernment, accountability, and a commitment to truth, fostering a society where information is a tool for enlightenment and understanding rather than division.

The Emergence of New Philosophies and Belief Systems

Baba Vanga's predictions for 2025 included a vision of new philosophies and belief systems emerging, reflecting humanity's quest for meaning, unity, and understanding in a rapidly changing world. She foresaw a future where traditional beliefs coexist with new, more holistic perspectives that integrate science, spirituality, and ethical values. Her prophecy suggested that these evolving belief systems would be driven by humanity's desire for purpose, community, and a deeper connection to nature and one another. In this chapter, we explore Baba Vanga's vision for the emergence of new philosophies, examining the forces driving this transformation and the potential impact on society and individual well-being.

A Shift toward Spiritual Inclusivity

Baba Vanga foresaw a shift toward more inclusive belief systems that draw from various religious, philosophical, and spiritual traditions. She envisioned individuals seeking wisdom from multiple sources, valuing insights from different faiths and cultural practices rather than adhering strictly to one tradition. Her vision included a growing openness to concepts like mindfulness, meditation, and the interconnectedness of all life, which transcend religious boundaries.

In her prophecy, Baba Vanga suggested that by embracing inclusive spirituality, people could cultivate a sense of unity and compassion, reducing divisiveness and promoting mutual respect. She believed that this blending of traditions would help humanity find common ground, fostering a world where diversity in beliefs is celebrated rather than a source of conflict.

Integration of Science and Spirituality

Baba Vanga predicted that the lines between science and spirituality would blur as people seek to understand the mysteries of life, consciousness, and the universe. She foresaw scientists and spiritual thinkers working together to explore questions about existence, consciousness, and the nature of reality. Her vision included breakthroughs in fields like quantum physics, neuroscience, and cosmology, which reveal the interconnectedness of all things and offer insights that align with ancient spiritual teachings.

Her prophecy suggested that these discoveries would inspire new philosophies that honor both scientific knowledge and spiritual wisdom. Baba Vanga believed that integrating science and spirituality would enable humanity to develop a more balanced worldview, fostering a sense of wonder, humility, and responsibility toward the planet and each other.

The Rise of Environmental and Earth-Centered Beliefs

Baba Vanga foresaw the rise of philosophies centered on environmentalism and a reverence for the Earth. She predicted that as people become more aware of ecological crises, they would adopt belief systems that emphasize living in harmony with nature. Her vision included practices that promote sustainability, conservation, and respect for all forms of life, viewing the Earth as a sacred entity deserving of care and protection.

In her prophecy, she saw people reconnecting with ancient practices, such as indigenous spirituality and earth-centered rituals, to find guidance on coexisting sustainably with the planet. Baba Vanga believed that these philosophies would instill a sense of collective responsibility and inspire individuals and communities to prioritize environmental stewardship as a core ethical value.

Philosophies Rooted in Compassion and Altruism

Baba Vanga's vision included the emergence of belief systems that prioritize compassion, kindness, and altruism as central values. She foresaw people embracing philosophies that encourage selflessness, empathy, and social responsibility, moving away from materialistic and self-centered lifestyles. Her prophecy suggested that by focusing on the well-being of others, individuals could find a sense of purpose and fulfillment, fostering a culture of generosity and mutual support.

In her vision, these compassionate philosophies would encourage individuals to see themselves as interconnected with all of humanity, inspiring acts of kindness, philanthropy, and service. Baba Vanga believed that this shift could create more cohesive and resilient communities, where people work together to support each other and uplift the vulnerable.

Emphasis on Personal Growth and Self-Discovery

Baba Vanga foresaw a growing interest in philosophies centered on personal growth, self-discovery, and inner transformation. She predicted that people would seek belief systems that encourage introspection, mindfulness, and the pursuit of inner peace. Her vision included practices like meditation, journaling, and therapy becoming widely accepted tools for self-reflection and emotional well-being.

Her prophecy suggested that by focusing on inner growth, individuals would develop greater self-awareness, emotional resilience, and a deeper understanding of their purpose. Baba Vanga believed that this shift toward self-discovery would lead to a more balanced society, where individuals are empowered to live authentically and in alignment with their values.

Digital-Age Philosophies and Virtual Communities

Baba Vanga foresaw the emergence of belief systems influenced by the digital age, with people connecting in virtual spaces to share ideas and philosophies. She predicted that online communities, forums, and social media would become platforms for exploring new beliefs, exchanging knowledge, and finding like-minded individuals. Her vision included digital communities fostering dialogue around ethical issues, environmental activism, and social justice, creating virtual spaces for collective learning and spiritual exploration.

In her prophecy, she recognized the potential for these virtual communities to bridge geographic and cultural divides, offering people a sense of belonging and connection. Baba Vanga believed that while digital platforms could facilitate the spread of meaningful ideas, it is essential for individuals to approach these spaces with discernment, balancing online engagement with real-world connections.

Global Ethics and Universal Values

Baba Vanga foresaw a future where new philosophies emphasize universal values, such as peace, equality, and justice, that transcend cultural and national boundaries. Her vision included a movement toward global ethics, where people recognize their shared responsibilities and ethical obligations to one another and the planet. She predicted that as humanity faces global challenges, people would be drawn to belief systems that encourage cooperation, understanding, and compassion for all.

Her prophecy suggested that these universal values would be rooted in a recognition of the inherent dignity of all people, regardless of background. Baba Vanga believed that by embracing these global ethics, humanity could create a foundation for a more harmonious world, where differences are respected and shared values are celebrated.

Challenges and Caution in Embracing New Philosophies

While Baba Vanga's vision for emerging belief systems was optimistic, she also warned of potential challenges. She foresaw the risk of superficial or commercialized spirituality, where meaningful practices are diluted or commodified. Her prophecy included concerns about individuals adopting beliefs without genuine understanding or commitment, resulting in confusion or inconsistency in values.

In her vision, Baba Vanga emphasized the importance of authenticity and discernment when exploring new philosophies. She believed that individuals should approach belief systems thoughtfully, seeking a deeper understanding and aligning their actions with their values. Her prophecy challenges people to honor the integrity of their beliefs, ensuring that they contribute positively to their lives and communities.

The Role of Education and Dialogue

Baba Vanga believed that education and open dialogue would play essential roles in the evolution of new belief systems. She foresaw schools, communities, and families encouraging respectful discussions about diverse philosophies, fostering a culture of curiosity and empathy. Her vision included the integration of ethics, philosophy, and mindfulness into educational curricula, helping young people develop a thoughtful approach to life's big questions.

Her prophecy suggested that by encouraging respectful dialogue, society could reduce prejudice, deepen mutual understanding, and create a more open-minded culture. Baba Vanga believed that when individuals are empowered to explore and understand different belief systems, they are better equipped to contribute to a peaceful and inclusive world.

Lessons from Baba Vanga's Prophecy

Baba Vanga's insights on the emergence of new philosophies and belief systems offer several key lessons for embracing these transformations with integrity and purpose:

- **Value Inclusivity:** Exploring diverse traditions can foster unity, respect, and a sense of shared purpose.
- **Integrate Science and Spirituality:** Balancing scientific understanding with spiritual wisdom creates a holistic approach to life's mysteries.
- **Prioritize Compassion and Altruism:** Emphasizing kindness, empathy, and service can enrich both individuals and communities.
- **Encourage Personal Growth:** Fostering self-awareness and personal development can lead to a more balanced, fulfilled society.
- **Practice Discernment:** Approaching new belief systems thoughtfully ensures that they contribute meaningfully to personal and social well-being.

Hope for an Enlightened Future

Baba Vanga's vision of emerging philosophies and belief systems reflects her belief in humanity's capacity for growth, empathy, and connection. She saw these evolving perspectives as an opportunity to transcend boundaries, embrace shared values, and create a world that honors the richness of human experience. Her prophecy suggests that by exploring new ways of understanding, humanity can cultivate a society that is rooted in wisdom, compassion, and unity.

As we continue to explore her predictions, Baba Vanga's insights remind us of the power of belief systems to shape our values, guide our actions, and inspire our collective journey. Her vision challenges us to seek truth, honor diversity, and build a future where new philosophies nurture both the individual and the global community.

Global Consciousness: The Unification of Minds and Souls

Baba Vanga's predictions for 2025 included a vision of humanity moving toward a unified global consciousness, where people transcend individual identities to connect through shared values, purpose, and empathy. She foresaw a world in which people increasingly experience a collective sense of responsibility, interconnectedness, and mutual understanding, fostering a sense of unity across borders, cultures, and beliefs. Her prophecy suggested that this awakening of global consciousness would be essential for addressing humanity's challenges and realizing its potential for peace, harmony, and progress. In this chapter, we explore Baba Vanga's vision of global consciousness, the forces driving this shift, and its implications for individuals and societies.

The Awakening of Global Consciousness

Baba Vanga foresaw a powerful awakening in human consciousness, with people increasingly aware of their shared humanity and the interconnectedness of all life. Her vision included individuals around the world feeling a deepened sense of empathy and responsibility toward one another and the planet. She believed that this awakening would create a shift in priorities, leading people to value collaboration, compassion, and harmony over competition and division.

In her prophecy, Baba Vanga suggested that this awakening would encourage people to seek meaning and fulfillment through acts of kindness, service, and a commitment to the greater good. She believed that by embracing a collective mindset, humanity could overcome challenges that once seemed insurmountable, building a world where the well-being of all is prioritized.

The Role of Technology in Connecting Minds

Baba Vanga envisioned technology playing a pivotal role in fostering global consciousness. She foresaw digital platforms, social networks, and virtual communities breaking down geographic barriers, enabling people from diverse backgrounds to connect, share experiences, and collaborate. Her vision included digital tools that facilitate cross-cultural dialogue, promote understanding, and support collective problem-solving.

However, Baba Vanga also cautioned that technology alone is not enough to create true unity. She believed that individuals must approach digital connections with openness, authenticity, and respect. Her prophecy suggested that while technology can be a powerful enabler of global consciousness, the depth and quality of human connections depend on the intentions and attitudes of the people using it.

Environmental Stewardship as a Unifying Force

Baba Vanga foresaw environmental issues as a major catalyst for the development of global consciousness. She believed that the urgent need to address climate change, protect biodiversity, and conserve resources would inspire people to transcend national, cultural, and economic divides. Her vision included a collective realization that humanity's fate is intertwined with the health of the planet, encouraging people to adopt sustainable practices and advocate for ecological responsibility.

In her prophecy, Baba Vanga saw environmental stewardship as a shared purpose that could unite humanity in a common cause. She believed that by recognizing their role as caretakers of the Earth, individuals would cultivate a sense of reverence for nature and a commitment to protecting future generations. Her vision suggests that this unity in purpose could be a powerful force for social cohesion and global progress.

The Emergence of Collective Empathy

Baba Vanga predicted that global consciousness would bring about a deep sense of collective empathy, where people become more attuned to the feelings and experiences of others. She foresaw individuals and communities developing a heightened ability to understand and relate to those facing different challenges, fostering a culture of compassion and support.

In her vision, collective empathy leads people to take action on behalf of the vulnerable, marginalized, and oppressed. Baba Vanga believed that this empathy-driven approach would transform societies, promoting policies and initiatives that prioritize social justice, human rights, and inclusivity. Her prophecy suggests that collective empathy could help bridge divides, reduce conflict, and create a more harmonious world.

Spirituality and the Quest for Unity

Baba Vanga foresaw spirituality playing a central role in the unification of minds and souls, with people increasingly seeking to connect to something greater than themselves. Her vision included individuals from various backgrounds embracing spiritual practices that emphasize compassion, mindfulness, and the interconnectedness of all life. She believed that this shift would encourage people to see themselves as part of a larger, universal whole.

In her prophecy, Baba Vanga suggested that spiritual practices like meditation, mindfulness, and contemplation would become widely adopted, helping people cultivate inner peace and a sense of unity. She believed that as individuals explore spirituality, they would find common ground across cultures and religions, fostering respect and understanding for diverse beliefs. Her vision suggests that spirituality could be a unifying force, helping humanity transcend material concerns and focus on shared values.

Education as a Pathway to Global Awareness

Baba Vanga believed that education would play a crucial role in fostering global consciousness. She foresaw schools and universities incorporating courses that emphasize global issues, ethics, and empathy, helping young people develop a sense of responsibility toward others. Her vision included educational initiatives that teach students about different cultures, environmental sustainability, and the interconnected nature of social issues.

Her prophecy suggested that by promoting a global perspective, education can empower individuals to act as informed, compassionate citizens of the world. Baba Vanga believed that education rooted in global awareness would help create a generation that values unity, cooperation, and respect for diversity.

Challenges and the Need for Patience

While Baba Vanga's vision of global consciousness was hopeful, she also foresaw challenges on the path to unity. She recognized that old divisions, prejudices, and self-centered attitudes could slow humanity's progress. Her prophecy included a reminder that fostering global consciousness requires patience, persistence, and the willingness to overcome resistance to change.

In her vision, Baba Vanga emphasized that true unity cannot be achieved through force or imposition but must arise organically through mutual understanding and voluntary cooperation. She believed that individuals and communities should be encouraged to embrace global consciousness at their own pace, fostering a sense of genuine connection and shared purpose.

Global Consciousness and Ethical Leadership

Baba Vanga foresaw that global consciousness would call for a new type of ethical leadership. She envisioned leaders who embody compassion, humility, and integrity, prioritizing the welfare of humanity and the planet over narrow interests. Her vision included leaders who inspire trust, promote inclusivity, and work collaboratively to address global challenges.

Her prophecy suggested that ethical leaders would play a key role in guiding humanity toward unity, fostering policies that reflect shared values and support global well-being. Baba Vanga believed that leaders who embrace global consciousness could inspire others to follow suit, creating a ripple effect that strengthens the bonds between nations and communities.

Lessons from Baba Vanga's Prophecy

Baba Vanga's insights on global consciousness offer several key lessons for cultivating unity and understanding in an interconnected world:

Embrace Empathy and Compassion: Developing a sense of empathy for others is essential for fostering unity and addressing shared challenges.

Utilize Technology for Connection: Leveraging digital tools responsibly can bridge divides and facilitate meaningful dialogue across cultures.

Prioritize Environmental Responsibility: Recognizing humanity's shared stake in the planet's health can unite people around a common cause.

Foster Spiritual Growth and Inclusivity: Embracing spirituality and shared values can promote respect and understanding across diverse beliefs.

Encourage Global Education: Teaching global awareness, ethics, and empathy can empower individuals to act as compassionate global citizens.

Hope for a Unified Humanity

Baba Vanga's vision of global consciousness is ultimately one of hope, suggesting that humanity has the capacity to transcend differences and come together in a spirit of unity and cooperation. She believed that by embracing empathy, compassion, and shared purpose, people can create a world where individual well-being is intertwined with the collective good. Her prophecy inspires humanity to seek understanding, value diversity, and recognize the power of connectedness.

As we conclude this chapter, Baba Vanga's insights challenge us to foster a global consciousness that honors the dignity, aspirations, and contributions of all people. Her vision reminds us that true unity arises not from uniformity, but from a recognition of our shared humanity and our potential to create a world rooted in harmony, compassion, and mutual respect.

Baba Vanga's Warning to Humanity: What Lies Ahead?

Baba Vanga's final prophecies for 2025 included a cautionary message to humanity, highlighting both the potential for progress and the risks of complacency. She foresaw a pivotal moment where the choices made by individuals, communities, and nations would shape the future of civilization. Her warning to humanity served as both a call to action and a reminder of the profound consequences of neglecting ethical responsibilities, environmental stewardship, and social harmony. In this chapter, we explore Baba Vanga's warning to humanity, examining the key themes of her message and the paths available for creating a sustainable, compassionate future.

The Urgency of Collective Responsibility

Baba Vanga's warning centered on the concept of collective responsibility, urging humanity to act with a sense of shared accountability for the planet and one another. She foresaw that by 2025, the interconnected nature of global issues would demand cooperation and a commitment to the common good. Her prophecy included an urgent call for individuals and leaders alike to consider the long-term impacts of their decisions on future generations.

In her vision, Baba Vanga emphasized that humanity must move beyond self-interest and short-term thinking. She believed that the key to overcoming major challenges lies in prioritizing collaboration, compassion, and a recognition of humanity's shared fate. Her warning suggests that only by embracing a sense of collective responsibility can humanity avoid the potential dangers that lie ahead.

Environmental Degradation and the Cost of Inaction

A major focus of Baba Vanga's warning was the ongoing degradation of the environment. She foresaw the possibility of severe consequences if humanity continues to exploit natural resources unsustainably, neglects the importance of biodiversity, and fails to address climate change. Her prophecy included vivid images of depleted ecosystems, extreme weather events, and scarcity of essential resources.

Baba Vanga's vision called for immediate action to restore ecological balance, warning that the cost of inaction would be irreversible damage to the planet. She believed that without a genuine commitment to environmental stewardship, humanity could face a future where nature's resilience is compromised, leading to widespread suffering and instability. Her message urges people to adopt sustainable practices, protect natural habitats, and view the planet as a shared home deserving of care and respect.

The Dangers of Misinformation and Erosion of Truth

Baba Vanga also warned of the dangers posed by misinformation, manipulation, and the erosion of truth. She foresaw a world where the rapid spread of false information could lead to confusion, fear, and division, hindering humanity's ability to make informed decisions. Her prophecy included concerns about the impact of biased media, echo chambers, and the use of technology to distort reality.

In her vision, Baba Vanga emphasized the importance of discerning truth, promoting media literacy, and upholding ethical standards in communication. She believed that the integrity of information is essential for maintaining social cohesion and fostering trust. Her warning suggests that by prioritizing truth and accountability, humanity can avoid the pitfalls of manipulation and create a foundation for genuine understanding.

The Threat of Social Fragmentation and Conflict

Baba Vanga's warning also addressed the risks of social fragmentation and conflict, which she foresaw as potential outcomes of unchecked inequality, prejudice, and political polarization. Her vision included images of communities divided by economic disparities, racial tensions, and ideological rifts, leading to distrust and unrest. She believed that these divides, if left unaddressed, could destabilize societies and hinder progress.

Her prophecy called for a renewed commitment to unity, inclusivity, and social justice. Baba Vanga believed that humanity must address the root causes of division, such as economic inequality and systemic discrimination, to foster a culture of respect and cooperation. Her warning suggests that only by embracing diversity and promoting fairness can society avoid the dangers of conflict and create a stable, harmonious future.

The Need for Ethical Leadership

Baba Vanga foresaw a future where ethical leadership would be critical in guiding humanity through its challenges. She warned of the risks posed by leaders driven by self-interest, corruption, or short-sighted ambitions. Her prophecy included a call for leaders who prioritize the well-being of the planet and its people, make decisions rooted in compassion, and approach power with humility and integrity.

In her vision, Baba Vanga believed that ethical leaders have the power to inspire positive change, foster trust, and promote unity. Her warning challenges societies to support leaders who demonstrate empathy, wisdom, and accountability. Baba Vanga's message suggests that ethical leadership is essential for navigating complex global issues and creating a future where progress benefits all.

Balancing Technological Advancement with Humanity

Baba Vanga warned of the potential risks associated with technological advancement if it is not balanced with humanity's ethical and social values. She foresaw the possibility of technology becoming a tool for control, surveillance, or exploitation, with people losing touch with their sense of humanity. Her vision included concerns about the over-reliance on technology, the ethical implications of AI, and the need for responsible innovation.

Her prophecy suggested that technology should serve as a tool to uplift humanity, not as a force that erodes human autonomy, privacy, or ethics. Baba Vanga believed that balancing technology with compassion, empathy, and ethical considerations would allow humanity to harness its benefits while avoiding its potential pitfalls. Her warning encourages people to use technology mindfully, with an emphasis on enhancing well-being and preserving human dignity.

The Promise of Unity and Transformation

While Baba Vanga's warning to humanity highlighted risks and challenges, she also foresaw the potential for profound transformation through unity and shared purpose. She believed that by coming together, embracing collective responsibility, and acting with integrity, humanity could achieve remarkable progress. Her vision included a world where people recognize their interconnectedness, support one another, and prioritize the greater good.

Baba Vanga's prophecy suggested that unity could empower humanity to overcome even the most daunting obstacles, creating a future marked by resilience, peace, and fulfillment. Her warning serves as a reminder that the power to shape the future lies within humanity's hands, and that the choices made today will define the world of tomorrow.

Lessons from Baba Vanga's Warning

Baba Vanga's final message to humanity offers several key lessons for creating a sustainable, ethical, and harmonious future:

- **Embrace Collective Responsibility:** Recognizing our interconnectedness can inspire actions that benefit both people and the planet.
- **Protect the Environment:** Taking immediate steps to address environmental issues is essential for ensuring a thriving future.
- **Prioritize Truth and Transparency:** Upholding truth in media and communication is crucial for fostering trust and understanding.
- **Promote Inclusivity and Social Justice:** Addressing inequality and embracing diversity can help create a stable, cohesive society.
- **Support Ethical Leadership:** Choosing leaders who demonstrate integrity, empathy, and a commitment to the common good is vital for positive change.
- **Balance Technology with Humanity:** Using technology responsibly and ethically can prevent its potential risks and enhance human well-being.

Hope for a Responsible Humanity

Baba Vanga's final warning to humanity is ultimately a message of hope and possibility. She believed that humanity has the capacity to learn from its mistakes, adapt, and make choices that lead to a brighter, more compassionate future. Her prophecy suggests that by heeding her warnings and embracing values of responsibility, unity, and empathy, humanity can create a world where peace, progress, and well-being are accessible to all. As we conclude her predictions, Baba Vanga's insights remind us of the profound impact that individual and collective actions have on the course of history. Her vision challenges us to rise to the occasion, to act with foresight and integrity, and to shape a future that honors the potential of all people and the beauty of the natural world.

Interpreting Baba Vanga's Predictions in Light of 2024 Events

As Baba Vanga's predictions for 2025 approach, reflecting on current events offers insight into how her prophecies may be unfolding. She foresaw a world at a crossroads, with both progress and peril on the horizon, and her predictions can provide a lens through which to interpret the challenges and transformations seen in 2024. In this chapter, we analyze Baba Vanga's predictions in light of significant events from 2024, exploring how they might foreshadow what lies ahead and what lessons they hold for humanity.

Climate-Driven Disasters and the Call for Environmental Stewardship

Baba Vanga's prediction of increasing natural disasters is evident in the extreme climate events witnessed throughout 2024. Record-breaking heatwaves, wildfires, hurricanes, and flooding have devastated communities worldwide, underscoring the urgent need for environmental stewardship. These events align with her warning about the cost of inaction on climate change, illustrating the fragility of natural ecosystems under pressure from human activities.

Her prophecy serves as a reminder that immediate action is required to curb environmental degradation. Efforts in 2024 toward sustainable energy, reforestation, and international climate agreements show positive steps, but her vision challenges humanity to accelerate these efforts and recognize the interconnectedness of environmental health and human prosperity.

Geopolitical Tensions and the Need for Unity

Baba Vanga foresaw a future where global unity was essential for addressing shared challenges, yet 2024 has been marked by escalating geopolitical tensions. Territorial disputes, shifting alliances, and conflicts over resources have intensified in several regions, reinforcing her prediction about the dangers of fragmentation. These divisions highlight the need for cooperative frameworks to address issues that no single nation can solve alone.

Her prophecy calls for diplomatic efforts that prioritize global well-being over narrow interests. In 2024, peace summits and international coalitions have shown promise in fostering dialogue, but Baba Vanga's vision reminds us that sustainable peace requires mutual respect, inclusivity, and a commitment to shared values. Her warning challenges leaders and citizens alike to work toward bridging divides and fostering unity.

The Rise of Artificial Intelligence and Technological Ethics

Baba Vanga predicted that technology would become a central force in shaping society, a prophecy that aligns with 2024's rapid advancements in artificial intelligence, automation, and digital tools. From generative AI to machine learning applications in healthcare, the potential benefits of technology are vast. However, ethical concerns around privacy, misinformation, and automation-induced job loss have also surfaced, reflecting Baba Vanga's warning about the need for responsible use of technology.

The events of 2024 reveal the importance of developing ethical frameworks to guide technological innovation. Her vision encourages humanity to balance innovation with ethical considerations, ensuring that technology enhances human well-being and respects privacy, autonomy, and integrity. As AI becomes more integrated into daily life, Baba Vanga's warning calls for vigilance, accountability, and transparency.

The Erosion of Truth and Media Accountability

Baba Vanga foresaw the erosion of truth as a potential threat to social cohesion, a concern that resonates with the prevalence of misinformation in 2024. Social media platforms, digital news outlets, and AI-generated content have made it difficult for people to discern fact from fiction, creating confusion and division. Her prophecy highlighted the risks of a world where truth becomes subjective, making public trust and media accountability crucial.

In response, 2024 has seen a growing emphasis on media literacy, fact-checking, and ethical journalism. Her vision suggests that sustaining a healthy information ecosystem depends on both creators and consumers acting responsibly. Baba Vanga's warning underscores the need to uphold truth and transparency as foundational values for an informed, cohesive society.

Social Justice Movements and the Push for Equality

Baba Vanga predicted a shift toward compassion, inclusivity, and social justice, a vision reflected in the social movements of 2024. Around the world, individuals and groups have advocated for gender equality, racial justice, LGBTQ+ rights, and workers' rights, highlighting the importance of fairness and inclusivity in shaping societies. Her prophecy suggests that prioritizing social justice is essential for creating stable, harmonious communities.

These movements show that while progress has been made, there is still work to be done. Baba Vanga's vision emphasizes the importance of empathy and respect for all people, challenging leaders and communities to dismantle systems of discrimination and create societies where everyone is valued. Her prophecy encourages individuals to recognize the role they play in promoting justice and fostering a sense of shared humanity.

Environmental Activism and the Growth of Earth-Centered Beliefs

Baba Vanga foresaw the rise of earth-centered philosophies, with people embracing belief systems that honor nature and prioritize sustainability. In 2024, environmental activism and the popularity of eco-spirituality have become powerful forces. Movements advocating for rewilding, plant-based diets, and zero-waste lifestyles have highlighted the value of ecological harmony.

These trends align with her vision of humanity developing a reverence for nature, seeking solutions that restore balance to the planet. Baba Vanga's prophecy suggests that reconnecting with nature is key to sustainable living and long-term survival. As more people adopt environmentally conscious practices, her vision challenges individuals to see themselves as stewards of the Earth, responsible for its care and preservation.

Health Crises and the Importance of Preparedness

Baba Vanga predicted future health crises, underscoring the need for vigilance and preparedness. The 2024 resurgence of infectious diseases and the strain on healthcare systems has reaffirmed the importance of resilient public health infrastructure. Her vision includes the necessity for countries to invest in medical research, preventative measures, and accessible healthcare.

In light of these events, Baba Vanga's warning calls for a proactive approach to health, one that includes early detection, community health education, and global cooperation. Her prophecy reminds humanity that prioritizing health is essential for social stability, urging leaders to prepare for the unexpected and safeguard the well-being of all people.

Economic Inequality and the Push for Ethical Leadership

Baba Vanga warned about the dangers of economic disparity, foreseeing that unchecked inequality could lead to social unrest and instability. The events of 2024, including inflation, housing crises, and labor disputes, have underscored the need for ethical economic policies that prioritize fairness and opportunity. Baba Vanga's prophecy calls for leaders who prioritize the common good and address the root causes of inequality.

Her warning challenges policymakers and corporate leaders to recognize the social impact of economic policies and to adopt ethical practices that uplift rather than exploit. In 2024, movements advocating for living wages, affordable housing, and social safety nets reflect a push for equitable systems that align with her vision of compassion and shared prosperity.

Lessons from Baba Vanga's Warnings and 2024 Events

Baba Vanga's predictions, viewed through the lens of 2024 events, offer several key lessons for navigating the future:

Embrace Environmental Responsibility: Recognizing the impact of climate-driven disasters and taking action to protect ecosystems are essential for a sustainable future.

Promote Unity Amid Geopolitical Tensions: Diplomatic efforts and shared goals can bridge divides and reduce the risk of conflict.

Balance Technological Advancement with Ethics: Prioritizing responsible innovation ensures that technology serves humanity rather than undermining it.

Protect the Integrity of Information: Ensuring media accountability and promoting media literacy are crucial for fostering an informed society.

Support Social Justice and Equality: Advocating for fairness and inclusivity creates resilient communities and reduces social divides.

Invest in Public Health: Preparedness and preventative healthcare measures are essential for protecting society against future health crises.

Prioritize Ethical Economic Policies: Addressing inequality and supporting ethical leadership can foster a fairer and more stable world.

Hope and Responsibility for the Future

Baba Vanga's warnings, alongside the lessons of 2024, remind us of the power of choice in shaping the future. Her prophecy offers a vision of hope tempered with responsibility, emphasizing that humanity has the capacity to create a world rooted in empathy, resilience, and ethical action. As we reflect on the events of 2024, Baba Vanga's insights challenge us to act with integrity, embrace our shared humanity, and strive for a future that honors the well-being of all life.

By heeding her warnings and learning from recent challenges, humanity can foster a world that embodies her vision—a world where unity, compassion, and progress lead us toward a brighter, more harmonious future.

Science and Prophecy: How Modern Data Aligns with Predictions

Baba Vanga's predictions for 2025 raise intriguing questions about how prophecy and scientific data intersect in shaping our understanding of the future. While prophecies are often rooted in visions and intuition, modern science uses data, observation, and analysis to project trends and potential outcomes. This chapter explores the alignment between Baba Vanga's predictions and recent scientific findings, examining how her foresight correlates with data-driven insights on climate, technology, health, and social dynamics. By exploring the parallels, we can better understand how prophecy and science might complement one another in offering humanity guidance.

Climate Change and Environmental Predictions

One of Baba Vanga's key predictions involved the increasing severity of climate-related events—something recent scientific studies also confirm. Climate science data has shown a clear trend of rising global temperatures, accelerating ice melt, more frequent extreme weather events, and biodiversity loss. Scientific projections for the coming years support her warnings about environmental degradation and underscore the urgency of climate action.

Scientific evidence also confirms her warnings about ecosystem collapse and species extinction. Biodiversity assessments reveal that species are disappearing at an alarming rate, with habitat loss, pollution, and climate change as primary causes. Baba Vanga's predictions echo what scientists emphasize: that without transformative environmental action, humanity risks destabilizing the planet's natural systems.

The Role of Technology in Society

Baba Vanga foresaw both the benefits and ethical dilemmas of advanced technology, particularly in fields like artificial intelligence, genetic modification, and digital communication. Modern data from technology research and development supports her vision of rapid advancements that carry both promise and potential risks. For example, AI has proven to be transformative across industries, but it also raises ethical questions around privacy, automation, and bias.

Studies on AI and machine learning align with her warning about the need for responsible innovation, showing that unregulated use of technology can lead to privacy breaches, misinformation, and job displacement. Scientific research supports her insights, emphasizing the need for ethical frameworks to guide AI development and ensure that technology enhances, rather than undermines, human well-being.

Health Crises and Global Preparedness

Baba Vanga's predictions regarding health crises resonate with current scientific findings that warn of potential global health threats. Epidemiologists have identified the conditions that make societies vulnerable to pandemics, including urbanization, global travel, environmental degradation, and antibiotic resistance. Recent pandemics, along with emerging diseases, highlight the risks she foresaw and underscore the need for investment in public health infrastructure and research.

Data from global health organizations supports her vision by showing the importance of early detection, vaccination, and international collaboration. Baba Vanga's warning calls for proactive measures, and scientific research confirms that preparedness, prevention, and accessible healthcare are crucial for protecting society from future health crises.

Social Fragmentation and the Psychology of Polarization

Baba Vanga's concerns about social fragmentation are mirrored by modern psychological and sociological studies on polarization, inequality, and mental health. Research shows that economic disparities, racial tensions, and ideological divisions have intensified in recent years, leading to increased social isolation, mistrust, and mental health challenges.

Scientific studies on the psychology of polarization reveal that people are more likely to form echo chambers in digital spaces, reinforcing biases and limiting exposure to differing perspectives. This research aligns with her warnings, suggesting that without efforts to bridge divides and promote empathy, society risks becoming more fractured. Social science insights support her call for unity, as studies show that inclusive policies and collaborative community efforts can foster resilience and reduce social divides.

Predictive Models in Environmental and Health Sciences

Baba Vanga's prophecies align with modern predictive modeling in both environmental science and epidemiology. Predictive models used by climate scientists, for example, forecast rising sea levels, shifting weather patterns, and resource shortages, all of which Baba Vanga foresaw as potential consequences of human activity. Similarly, predictive models in epidemiology use data on disease transmission, vaccination rates, and global travel patterns to anticipate outbreaks and potential pandemics.

These models rely on statistical analysis, machine learning, and real-time data to predict future scenarios—tools that, while different from Baba Vanga's intuitive insights, reach similar conclusions about the risks of environmental neglect and unpreparedness for health crises. Her warnings, reinforced by data-driven models, serve as reminders of the importance of planning and preventive action.

The Quest for Truth in a Misinformation Age

Baba Vanga's warnings about misinformation and the erosion of truth find strong parallels in recent studies on the impact of misinformation and digital media on society. Research shows that the spread of false information can distort public perception, fuel political polarization, and hinder informed decision-making. Social scientists have also studied the psychological effects of misinformation, noting that repeated exposure to false information can lead people to believe in its accuracy—a phenomenon known as the "illusory truth effect."

Data from media and communication studies aligns with her vision, showing that safeguarding truth is essential for maintaining social cohesion and public trust. Baba Vanga's warning about the importance of transparency and media accountability reflects the findings of researchers who emphasize the need for fact-checking, media literacy, and responsible journalism.

Advances in Neuroscience and Consciousness Studies

Baba Vanga predicted a future where humanity gains a deeper understanding of consciousness and interconnectedness. Interestingly, advances in neuroscience, psychology, and consciousness studies have begun to shed light on the mysteries of human perception, self-awareness, and the effects of meditation and mindfulness on the brain. Research into consciousness has shown that practices like mindfulness can enhance empathy, reduce stress, and improve mental health.

Her vision of a global consciousness aligns with findings in neuroscience, which suggest that cultivating compassion and mindfulness can foster a sense of unity and interconnectedness. Studies on neuroplasticity reveal that intentional practices can reshape the brain's neural pathways, supporting her belief that humanity has the potential to evolve in ways that promote harmony and empathy.

Interpreting Science and Prophecy: Complementary Insights

While prophecy and science may seem like opposing approaches, Baba Vanga's predictions and modern scientific insights often reach similar conclusions about the challenges and opportunities humanity faces. Her prophecies, rooted in intuition, serve as cautionary messages, while scientific data provides concrete evidence and solutions. By interpreting these insights together, we can gain a more holistic understanding of humanity's trajectory and the steps necessary for a sustainable future.

Scientific data supports many of her key themes, including environmental stewardship, social unity, ethical use of technology, and the need for truth and transparency. Her warnings and scientific evidence together remind humanity that responsible action, compassion, and a commitment to truth are essential for thriving in an increasingly interconnected world.

Lessons from Science and Prophecy for a Balanced Future

Baba Vanga's prophecies and modern science offer complementary perspectives on navigating the future. Together, they provide several lessons for building a balanced, ethical, and resilient society:

Act on Climate Science: Scientific data supports her environmental warnings, urging humanity to take decisive action to protect ecosystems and address climate change.

Embrace Ethical Innovation: Both her prophecies and scientific findings emphasize the importance of responsible technology use, prioritizing human well-being and privacy.

Prepare for Health Challenges: Epidemiological research supports her warning about health crises, highlighting the need for preparedness, early detection, and global cooperation.

Promote Social Cohesion: Studies on polarization align with her vision of unity, suggesting that inclusive policies and empathy can reduce social divides.

Safeguard Truth and Media Integrity: Data on misinformation supports her concerns, emphasizing the importance of transparency, fact-checking, and media literacy.

Cultivate Compassion and Global Awareness: Neuroscientific research aligns with her vision of global consciousness, highlighting the potential for mindfulness to foster empathy and connectedness.

Hope for a Harmonious Future

Baba Vanga's prophecies, interpreted alongside scientific findings, remind us of the power of informed action guided by wisdom and foresight. Her vision of unity, responsibility, and compassion finds support in data-driven insights, suggesting that humanity has both the intuition and the knowledge to build a sustainable future. By integrating scientific understanding with a commitment to ethical principles, humanity can achieve a balance that honors both the practical and the profound.

As we reflect on her predictions and modern data, Baba Vanga's insights offer a hopeful message: that by heeding both intuitive wisdom and scientific evidence, humanity can create a future where technology serves life, truth fosters unity, and compassion guides progress. Her vision challenges us to move forward with purpose, embracing the tools of science while honoring the values that sustain the human spirit.

Reflections on Baba Vanga's 2025 and Beyond

As we approach 2025, Baba Vanga's predictions resonate with a new depth, illuminating the hopes and challenges that lie ahead for humanity. Her visions have offered a compelling blend of caution and optimism, suggesting that humanity stands on the cusp of significant transformation. Reflecting on her prophecies—particularly those extending beyond 2025—encourages us to consider how our actions today shape the trajectory of future generations. In this chapter, we reflect on Baba Vanga's insights, exploring their potential implications for the future and the lasting legacy of her wisdom.

2025 as a Turning Point: The Crossroads of Choice

Baba Vanga often referred to the mid-2020s as a pivotal era, a time when humanity must decide between paths of unity and division, environmental responsibility and neglect, truth and misinformation. Her vision of 2025 as a turning point is both a call to action and a reminder that humanity's collective choices will have enduring impacts. As we reflect on her prophecies, it becomes clear that this era may represent more than a passing phase; it could be a critical juncture in which humanity defines its values and priorities for the future.

Her predictions encourage us to recognize that the decisions made in the next few years—around climate action, social cohesion, technological ethics, and global health—will shape the kind of world we leave for future generations. Baba Vanga's vision serves as an invitation to act consciously, fostering a mindset that prioritizes resilience, responsibility, and empathy.

The Long-Term Vision: A Future of Unity and Understanding

Looking beyond 2025, Baba Vanga's prophecies suggest a future where humanity moves toward unity, compassion, and a shared sense of purpose. She foresaw a world where technological advances are guided by ethical frameworks, environmental stewardship is central to societal values, and individuals embrace a global consciousness that transcends national and cultural boundaries. Her vision is one of hope, highlighting humanity's potential for growth and transformation.

In imagining this future, Baba Vanga emphasizes the need for humility, open-mindedness, and a willingness to learn from past mistakes. Her predictions for the distant future reveal a world where people prioritize harmony with one another and with nature, embracing diversity and honoring the interconnectedness of all life. This vision challenges us to cultivate qualities like patience, respect, and cooperation—values that can guide us toward a sustainable, peaceful future.

The Role of Youth in Shaping the Future

Baba Vanga's prophecies often hinted at the importance of younger generations in driving change. She believed that the youth of today would be the architects of tomorrow's world, bringing fresh perspectives, creativity, and a passion for justice. Reflecting on her predictions encourages us to consider the role of education, mentorship, and empowerment in preparing future generations to lead with integrity and compassion.

Her vision for the future suggests that nurturing young people with the skills, knowledge, and values needed to tackle global challenges is essential. Investing in education that emphasizes critical thinking, environmental awareness, empathy, and ethical reasoning can ensure that future leaders are equipped to make decisions that prioritize both progress and humanity. Baba Vanga's insights remind us that empowering youth is key to a resilient, adaptable world.

Technology as a Tool for Good or Harm

Baba Vanga foresaw the transformative potential of technology and its dual capacity for both positive and negative outcomes. She envisioned a world where technology could either elevate humanity, facilitating connection, discovery, and problem-solving, or it could serve as a tool for division, control, and alienation. Her reflections on technology serve as a reminder that humanity must approach innovation with wisdom and caution.

Beyond 2025, her vision suggests that our relationship with technology will determine much about the quality of life and societal values in the future. Baba Vanga challenges us to ensure that technological advances respect privacy, preserve autonomy, and support ethical goals. By using technology to amplify our capacity for compassion, sustainability, and cooperation, we can realize its full potential as a force for good.

Environmental Stewardship as a Foundational Value

Baba Vanga consistently warned of the consequences of environmental neglect and emphasized the importance of harmony between humanity and nature. Her long-term vision for the future includes a society where environmental stewardship is woven into the fabric of daily life, and where people understand their role as caretakers of the Earth. Reflecting on her predictions inspires us to prioritize ecological balance, viewing sustainability not as a trend but as an enduring responsibility.

In a future shaped by ecological values, individuals and communities recognize that their actions impact the well-being of all living things. Baba Vanga's prophecies remind us that the health of the planet is interconnected with human prosperity, urging us to protect natural resources, restore habitats, and adopt lifestyles that respect the Earth's limits.

The Emergence of Global Ethics and Compassion

A key theme in Baba Vanga's predictions for the future is the rise of a global ethical framework rooted in compassion, respect, and inclusivity. She envisioned a world where ethical values guide decision-making on an individual and collective level, fostering societies that are just, fair, and inclusive. Her vision highlights the importance of empathy, mutual respect, and a sense of shared humanity as guiding principles.

Her prediction for the rise of global ethics suggests a future where individuals see themselves as part of a larger whole, acting not only for personal gain but for the benefit of all. Baba Vanga's insights remind us that achieving such a world requires both personal accountability and institutional transformation. By promoting education, dialogue, and ethical governance, we can lay the foundation for a compassionate and inclusive global community.

Learning from the Past to Build a Resilient Future

Reflecting on Baba Vanga's prophecies encourages us to learn from history, understanding that past mistakes need not be repeated if we approach the future with humility and foresight. Her insights suggest that resilience comes from acknowledging vulnerabilities, embracing diversity, and remaining adaptable in the face of change. By applying lessons from the past, humanity can build a future that is both innovative and grounded in enduring values.

Her vision challenges us to appreciate the strength in resilience and to approach the future with a balanced mindset, one that values both progress and preservation. Baba Vanga believed that by honoring the wisdom of those who came before us while embracing the possibilities of tomorrow, humanity can find a path forward that is both hopeful and secure.

Reflections and Hope for Humanity's Future

As we look beyond 2025, Baba Vanga's prophecies leave us with a hopeful yet cautionary message. She believed that humanity possesses the wisdom, creativity, and compassion needed to overcome its challenges, yet the outcome depends on the choices we make each day. Her vision for the future is one where people live in harmony with each other and the planet, embracing a shared sense of purpose that transcends individual interests.

Reflecting on her insights offers hope that, despite the obstacles we face, humanity can forge a path toward unity, sustainability, and peace. Baba Vanga's prophecies remind us of the immense potential within each person to contribute positively to the world, challenging us to embody the values of kindness, empathy, and responsibility.

Lessons for the Future from Baba Vanga's Prophecies

Baba Vanga's vision of 2025 and beyond provides several guiding principles for navigating the journey ahead:

Prioritize Unity and Empathy: Embracing diversity and promoting inclusivity can foster resilience and strengthen communities.

Protect the Planet: Viewing environmental stewardship as a core value ensures that future generations inherit a thriving Earth.

Advance Technology Responsibly: Using innovation to enhance human well-being requires ethical frameworks that prioritize privacy, autonomy, and dignity.

Support Ethical Leadership: Leaders who demonstrate compassion, integrity, and humility can inspire meaningful change and build trust.

Empower Future Generations: Investing in education, mentorship, and opportunities for young people ensures a brighter, more resilient future.

Foster a Global Ethical Mindset: Emphasizing compassion, respect, and shared purpose can help humanity navigate complex challenges with integrity.

Hope and Responsibility as Humanity's Guiding Stars

Baba Vanga's reflections on the future challenge us to embrace both hope and responsibility as guiding stars. Her vision reminds us that humanity's future is not predetermined; it is shaped by the actions, choices, and values we hold dear. By aligning with the principles of unity, compassion, and stewardship, humanity can create a world that reflects the highest aspirations of all people.

As we approach 2025 and look toward the future beyond, Baba Vanga's insights inspire us to act with courage, wisdom, and an unwavering commitment to the well-being of all. Her prophecies are not just predictions; they are an invitation to build a future where peace, progress, and harmony define the human experience.

Baba Vanga's Prophecies about Donald Trump in 2025

Baba Vanga's prophecies have long captured global attention for their enigmatic nature and perceived connections to significant political figures, including former U.S. President Donald Trump. Her visions often interpreted through metaphorical or symbolic lenses, have been linked to key moments in his political career. For 2025, Baba Vanga's predictions about Trump point toward themes of power, influence, and the impact of leadership during a time of global transition.

In this chapter, we explore how Baba Vanga's prophecies align with events and conditions surrounding Donald Trump, interpreting the implications of her visions for the political and social dynamics of 2025.

The Trump Legacy: A Divisive Figure

Donald Trump's presidency and subsequent role in American politics have been characterized by polarization. Baba Vanga's prophecies have often alluded to figures who disrupt traditional power structures, bringing about dramatic shifts in governance and public opinion. These descriptions resonate with Trump's influence, particularly his ability to galvanize supporters while facing intense opposition.

For 2025, Baba Vanga predicted challenges arising from leadership that tests the resilience of democratic institutions. This could be interpreted as a reflection of Trump's ongoing influence on American politics, whether as a political candidate, party leader, or cultural figure. Her prophecy suggests that such leaders have the potential to redefine norms but also carry the risk of deepening societal divisions.

A Leader "Surrounded by Storms"

One of Baba Vanga's symbolic visions described a leader "surrounded by storms, yet still standing tall." This imagery has often been associated with Donald Trump, whose tenure and post-presidency have been marked by controversy, legal battles, and political resilience. In 2025, this prophecy could signify continued challenges in Trump's orbit—whether political, legal, or societal—but also his enduring presence in shaping discourse and policy.

The "storms" may also represent broader crises, such as economic instability, international tensions, or domestic unrest, where Trump's influence plays a role in responses or solutions. Baba Vanga's vision challenges us to consider how such figures navigate adversity and the impact of their choices on broader societal dynamics.

Global Leadership and Influence

Baba Vanga's prophecies often extend beyond individual leaders to the global implications of their actions. For 2025, her predictions hint at significant shifts in international alliances and power dynamics. Trump's "America First" policy during his presidency redefined U.S. relationships with allies and adversaries, and his enduring influence could continue to shape these dynamics.

Her vision of "a voice that echoes across oceans" could symbolize a leader whose policies and rhetoric influence not only their own nation but also the global stage. In 2025, this might manifest through Trump's alignment with or opposition to global initiatives on trade, climate change, or geopolitical stability. Baba Vanga's prophecy underscores the interconnectedness of leadership and the world's evolving political landscape.

The Challenge of Reconciliation

Another theme in Baba Vanga's prophecies is the potential for reconciliation or further division under polarizing leaders. For 2025, her predictions point to a critical need for healing in societies fractured by ideological divides. This aligns with Trump's role as a figure who evokes strong loyalty and equally strong opposition, raising questions about his influence on unity or discord within the U.S.

Her prophecy invites reflection on how leadership can either bridge gaps or widen them. It challenges leaders and citizens alike to consider paths toward understanding and collaboration, even amid stark differences.

Interpretations and Speculations

While Baba Vanga's prophecies are open to interpretation, their alignment with Donald Trump's trajectory highlights the complexities of leadership in turbulent times. Her visions for 2025 suggest a world grappling with change, where the actions of influential figures have far-reaching consequences.

Baba Vanga's prophecies encourage us to look beyond the individual to the systems and values that leaders embody. Whether Trump's role in 2025 is one of active political engagement or symbolic influence, her predictions serve as a reminder of the enduring impact of leadership on the collective psyche and future of nations.

Lessons from Baba Vanga's Prophecies

Baba Vanga's insights into leadership and figures like Donald Trump offer several lessons for navigating the complexities of modern politics:

The Importance of Accountability: Leaders' actions have consequences that ripple across societies, making accountability essential for progress.

Unity amid Division: Leadership must prioritize reconciliation and understanding to foster social cohesion in polarized times.

Global Responsibility: Decisions made by influential figures affect not only their nations but also the global community, requiring ethical and collaborative approaches.

Adaptation and Resilience: Navigating "storms" requires adaptability and a commitment to long-term well-being over short-term gains.

A Reflection on Leadership and Legacy

As we consider Baba Vanga's prophecies about Donald Trump and 2025, we are reminded of the profound influence leaders wield and the enduring nature of their legacies. Her visions challenge us to reflect on the qualities we value in leadership and the responsibilities that come with power. Whether through direct action or symbolic presence, Trump's role in shaping the political and social landscape continues to evoke questions about the path forward for both the U.S. and the world.

Baba Vanga's insights offer a vision of possibility—one where leaders, guided by wisdom and responsibility, can navigate challenges to create a future defined by unity, progress, and hope.

Conclusion: What Does Baba Vanga's Legacy Mean for Our Future?

Baba Vanga's legacy offers more than a set of predictions; it serves as a profound reflection on humanity's potential, choices, and the values that guide our journey forward. Her insights, spanning environmental stewardship, social harmony, ethical leadership, and global consciousness, highlight the challenges and opportunities humanity faces. In this final chapter, we explore what Baba Vanga's legacy means for our future, reflecting on how her wisdom and cautionary messages can inspire a vision of hope, unity, and responsibility for generations to come.

The Enduring Relevance of Prophecy and Intuition

Baba Vanga's legacy reminds us of the power of prophecy and intuition as tools for guiding humanity. While science and logic play crucial roles in understanding the world, Baba Vanga's intuitive insights offer a different, equally valuable perspective—one that taps into timeless wisdom, spiritual depth, and an instinct for the interconnectedness of all life. Her legacy encourages us to balance scientific knowledge with an openness to intuition, honoring both as sources of insight and guidance.

In a world increasingly focused on data and technology, Baba Vanga's life teaches us that wisdom can emerge from unexpected places. Her ability to see beyond the present moment challenges us to respect diverse ways of knowing and to seek answers that integrate both logic and intuition.

A Legacy of Responsibility and Ethical Action

Central to Baba Vanga's prophecies is the idea of responsibility—responsibility to each other, to the planet, and to future generations. Her legacy challenges individuals and leaders to approach the future with a mindset rooted in ethics and compassion. She believed that every person plays a role in shaping the future, and her warnings about environmental degradation, social injustice, and ethical lapses serve as reminders of the consequences of inaction and apathy.

Her legacy encourages us to ask questions about the ethical dimensions of our actions. Are we acting in ways that uplift and protect one another? Are we considering the long-term impact of our choices? Baba Vanga's insights inspire a future where humanity collectively commits to acting responsibly, recognizing that our actions today shape the world we leave behind.

Environmental Stewardship as a Moral Imperative

Baba Vanga's deep respect for nature and her warnings about environmental destruction underscore the importance of ecological consciousness. Her legacy challenges us to view environmental stewardship as a moral duty, not a mere option. She reminds us that humanity's well-being is inseparably linked to the health of the planet, and that we must protect it to ensure a sustainable future.

In a world facing climate change, biodiversity loss, and pollution, her insights serve as a timeless call to action. Baba Vanga's legacy encourages individuals, communities, and nations to make sustainable choices, protect natural habitats, and embrace lifestyles that respect the Earth's limits. By honoring her message, we can foster a future where nature and humanity coexist harmoniously.

Unity and Global Consciousness: Embracing Our Shared Humanity

One of the most profound aspects of Baba Vanga's legacy is her vision of global consciousness—a world where individuals transcend cultural, national, and religious boundaries to recognize their shared humanity. Her prophecies reflect a future where unity and empathy are guiding values, fostering societies that prioritize peace, inclusivity, and mutual respect.

In an era often marked by division, her legacy reminds us of the strength that lies in diversity and the power of compassion to bridge differences. Baba Vanga's vision challenges us to cultivate empathy, to approach conflicts with understanding, and to build a future that reflects our interconnectedness. Her legacy serves as an enduring call to create a world where everyone has a sense of belonging and dignity.

The Pursuit of Truth and Transparency

Baba Vanga's warnings about misinformation and the erosion of truth highlight the importance of transparency and integrity in a rapidly evolving media landscape. Her legacy encourages individuals to seek truth, to question sources, and to hold media accountable for accurate, ethical reporting. She recognized that a society grounded in truth is essential for informed decision-making, social cohesion, and democracy.

Her legacy inspires a commitment to truth, both in media and in personal lives. By valuing honesty, clarity, and accuracy, we can build a culture that respects truth as a fundamental pillar of progress and unity. Baba Vanga's insights challenge humanity to create information systems that empower, rather than deceive, fostering a future where people are equipped to make choices that benefit society as a whole.

A Call for Ethical Leadership and Compassionate Governance

Baba Vanga's prophecies consistently emphasized the need for ethical leadership, highlighting the influence that leaders have over humanity's fate. Her legacy encourages the cultivation of leaders who prioritize the common good, act with integrity, and approach governance with humility and empathy. She believed that leaders have a moral obligation to protect the vulnerable, uplift communities, and safeguard the planet.

In today's complex world, her legacy calls for leaders who inspire trust, embody justice, and act transparently. By supporting leaders who reflect these values, society can work toward a future where governance promotes peace, fairness, and sustainability. Baba Vanga's vision challenges humanity to demand ethical leadership and to empower those who dedicate themselves to the well-being of all.

Empowering Future Generations with Baba Vanga's Wisdom

Baba Vanga's legacy extends to younger generations, whom she saw as catalysts for change and transformation. Her insights encourage the education and empowerment of youth, equipping them with the knowledge, skills, and values needed to address global challenges. By fostering curiosity, compassion, and resilience, her legacy can inspire future leaders, thinkers, and creators who are committed to building a better world.

Her vision reminds us that investing in young people is essential for a sustainable future. By providing education that emphasizes critical thinking, environmental responsibility, and empathy, we honor Baba Vanga's legacy, ensuring that future generations inherit both the wisdom of the past and the tools to create positive change.

Reflecting on Hope and Responsibility

Baba Vanga's legacy is ultimately one of hope tempered with responsibility. Her prophecies reveal the risks of ignoring our ethical duties, but they also offer a vision of humanity's potential for greatness, kindness, and resilience. She believed that while the path forward may be challenging, it is also filled with opportunities to act with integrity and compassion.

As we consider her legacy, we are reminded that hope is not a passive emotion but a call to action. Baba Vanga's insights inspire us to approach the future with courage and clarity, recognizing that we each play a part in creating the world we envision. Her legacy encourages us to take ownership of our actions, to seek solutions grounded in empathy, and to strive for a future where humanity's highest aspirations are realized.

Lessons from Baba Vanga's Legacy for a Brighter Future

Reflecting on Baba Vanga's life and predictions offers several guiding principles for building a sustainable, peaceful, and harmonious world:

Balance Intuition with Knowledge: Valuing both science and intuition allows us to approach the future with a holistic perspective.

Embrace Responsibility: Recognizing our duty to each other, the planet, and future generations is essential for meaningful progress.

Promote Ethical Leadership: Supporting leaders who embody compassion, integrity, and transparency can guide humanity toward a positive future.

Foster Unity and Global Consciousness: Embracing diversity and mutual respect strengthens communities and promotes peace.

Protect Truth and Integrity: Valuing transparency and accountability creates a society grounded in trust and informed decision-making.

Empower Future Generations: Educating young people with empathy and resilience ensures a hopeful and capable future.

A Vision of a Compassionate, Sustainable Future

Baba Vanga's legacy leaves us with an inspiring vision: a world where humanity acts with integrity, respects the Earth, and honors the dignity of all people. Her insights are a call to align our choices with our values, to foster resilience in the face of challenges, and to cultivate a spirit of unity that transcends borders and divisions. Her legacy is a reminder that each person has the power to make a difference, to contribute positively, and to create a future where compassion, sustainability, and peace guide our collective journey.

As we conclude our exploration of her predictions, Baba Vanga's wisdom serves as both a map and a mirror, challenging us to reflect on who we are and who we aspire to become. Her legacy offers us the tools to navigate the uncertainties of tomorrow with hope, purpose, and an unwavering commitment to the well-being of all.

I hope you found wisdom here and hope for our future. If you liked this book, please leave a review where you bought it. Thank you from the author.

About the Author

Andrew Parry is a writer whose fascination with the great thinkers, philosophers, and the nature of reality deeply influences his work. His writing is shaped by an enduring curiosity about the fundamental questions of existence—what it means to be human, how we understand the world around us, and the intricate relationships between thought, perception, and reality. Through his exploration of these themes, Andrew seeks to provoke thoughtful reflection and open new pathways of understanding for his readers.

Read more at https://lonetrail.blog.